YORK FILM NOTES

The Terminator

Director
James Cameron

Note by Nigel Whittaker

Longman   EG15149   York Press

York Press
322 Old Brompton Road, London SW5 9JH

Pearson Education Limited
Edinburgh Gate, Harlow, Essex CM20 2JE, United Kingdom
Associated companies, branches and representatives throughout
the world

First published 2000

ISBN 0-582-43186-7

Designed by Vicki Pacey
Phototypeset by Gem Graphics, Trenance, Mawgan Porth, Cornwall
Colour reproduction and film output by Spectrum Colour
Printed in Malaysia, KVP

contents

acknowledgement To Al and Jack for help
and dedication above and beyond.

———///———

author of this note Nigel Whittaker graduated from
Stirling University, where he studied Film as part of his course in English
Studies. He has been teaching English since 1987.

THE TERMINATOR **y**

background

trailer

The gladiatorial arena is set, with vulnerable flesh and cunning verses a leviathan who totes around massive weapons like so many chic accessories and can rebuild his organs as they get shot away. The pacing and the action are terrific, revelling in the feral relentlessness which characterised *Assault on Precinct 13* and *Mad Max 2*, even the future visions of a wasted LA are well mounted. More than enough violence to make it a profoundly moral film; and Arnold's a whizz.

Time Out

A non-stop Odyssey of perpetual motion with vivid characterisation, unflagging tension, superb stunts and a meaty story line.

Empire

No amount of flip humour can compensate for the film's mindless cruelty.

The Times

A blazing, cinematic comic book full of virtuoso moviemaking, terrific momentum, solid performances and a compelling story.

Variety

Slick, rather nasty but undeniably compelling comic book adventure.

Halliwell's

The Terminator has an echoing mythic story, a raw, gutsy Linda Hamilton, Schwarzenegger cast with flair and humour, and a relaxed, economical air.

David Thomson, Biographical Dictionary of Film

reading the terminator

In 1984 a director, who had been fired from his previous film (which was his directional debut – a B-movie shocker about flying piranha) came together with a world-renowned body-builder, hot off his second starring movie role in a sword and sorcery fantasy. With a cast of relatively unknown actors and a modest budget the aim was to make a science fiction action adventure film, the idea for which was born in an hallucinatory dream as the director, suffering from depression, lay impoverished and feverish with a bad case of the flu in a hotel in Rome, where he had illegally been trying to recut the disastrous debut.

Certainly the omens were not good, even the films distributors had few expectations, but such is the stuff of Hollywood legend and lore that upon release the film, whose production costs amounted to a cautious $6.4 million, became an instant box office smash taking up to $40 million in the USA alone, moving to $100 million in worldwide ticket sales and later attracting an enormous audience with its release on video. The critics too were not ungenerous, with the film making many of the critics' top ten lists, being voted the most important film of the 1980s by *Esquire* magazine and finding itself canonised by the British Film institute with its 1996 publication in the *Modern Classics* series.

For the writer/director James Cameron the film launched his career, simultaneously helping him recover from the debacle that was *Piranha 2: The Spawning* and firmly establishing him in the vanguard of action adventure directors in a career that, after six films in a thirteen year period, found him sweeping the board at the Academy Awards, earning himself an Oscar for Best Director, whilst his film *Titanic* was named best film.

Cameron credits some of *The Terminator*'s success to the audience reaction to Arnold Schwarzenegger, its body-building star. 'Its fun to fantasize being a guy who can do whatever he wants ... Arnold is indestructible' (Perlman, 1985, p. 36).

Schwarzenegger was originally selected to play the character of Reese, the time-travelling hero of the film, but, whether at Cameron's suggestion or Schwarzenegger's insistence – such is the film's lore, he took the role of villain as the Terminator. Having found worldwide success in his body-building career, Schwarzenegger had further added to his star status with *Conan the Barbarian* (1981) and *Conan the Destroyer* (1984) despite their lack of financial success, but with *The Terminator* Arnold, 'Arnie' to his adoring fans, was catapulted into the highest echelons of movie stardom in a role that has proved so influential that even today his name is synonymous with the character.

In order to appreciate further the success and influence of *The Terminator* it should be seen in the context of its genre; that being a hybrid of action adventure and science fiction. In *The Encyclopedia of Science Fiction* John Clute and Peter Nicholls chart the rise of science fiction cinema from 1968 onwards, identifying a move from the visually and intellectually audacious *2001: A Space Odyssey* to the opening of the commercial floodgates brought about in the late 1970s / early 1980s by the *Star Wars* films and *Close Encounters of the Third Kind*.

'In 1971 the cinema of the fantastic ... accounted for about 5 per cent of the US box office takings, by 1982 this figure had risen amazingly to approach 50 per cent, and it remained as high as about 30 per cent in 1990' (Clute and Nicholls, p. 223). In their *Encyclopedia*, Clute and Nicholls award *The Terminator* the best of the killer robot sub-genre that includes *Saturn 3* (1980) and *Android* (1982). The success of *The Terminator* is most probably a significant factor in the spate of such films that followed in its wake: *Robocop* (1987), *Hardware, Class of 1999, Robocop 2* and *Robot Jox* (all 1990), and *Eve of Destruction* (1991).

The film's science fiction themes, namely human beings versus machines and time travel, are central to the story line, but its momentum and the plethora of spectacular action scenes firmly place *The Terminator* in the action adventure trend, which came to prominence in the 1980s and lasted well into the 1990s, forming the staple diet of the summer blockbuster. Indeed *The Terminator* stands at the vanguard of this trend, alongside *Alien* (1979), the first instalment of Sylvester Stallone's *Rambo* films, *First Blood* (1982) and the first of Steven Spielberg's Indiana Jones films, *Raiders of the Lost Ark* (1982). In the masculine world of action adventure the film more than fulfilled the genre conventions in the imposing figure of provides a strong female lead

Schwarzenegger, but also stretched those conventions in providing a strong role for its female lead Linda Hamilton, who would come to stand alongside Sigourney Weaver, whose Ripley in *Alien* had already demonstrated that women were there to assert themselves alongside their male lead counterparts.

Whilst acknowledging that, first and foremost, a film like *The Terminator* is primarily about entertaining an audience, Cameron goes on to imbue his film with meanings that have become the subject of lasting debate:

> The producer, Gail Hurd, and I set out to make a movie that would function on a couple of levels: as a linear action piece that a 12 year old would think was the most mad picture he had ever seen, and as science fiction that a 45 year old Stanford English Prof. would think had some sort of socio-political significance between the lines although obviously it doesn't attempt to be that primarily.
>
> Cameron in French, The Terminator, 1996, p. 47

In his highly entertaining and illuminating *BFI Modern Classics* guide to the film Sean French (1996) takes Cameron at his word and attempts to see the film from that Stanford English professor's point of view. Regardless of age or professional qualification the 'significance between the lines' has been hotly debated from the Internet to cinematic journal. Such readings have sought to see the film in religious terms, as a feminist subversion of an essentially male genre and even as an anti-establishment manifesto.

key players' biographies

ARNOLD SCHWARZENEGGER

This seemingly indestructible body is, as *Time* observed, 'its own stunning special effect'. The sloping planes of his smooth, simian features are as chiselled as a comic book super hero. He is the blockbuster given human – or at least humanoid – form. Mapped, quantified, evaluated, the Schwarzenegger torso is less a sex object than an object lesson, recapitulating the post-Renaissance transformation of the human body into something to be

> manipulated and rationalised, surveyed and regulated, subjugated
> to the institutional discipline of prisons, schools, hospitals.
>
> Hoberman, 1991, p. 22

The body is in many respects Schwarzenegger's trademark; a carefully crafted special effect honed over a long period of time into a vehicle for escape and a means of realising dreams.

Born in Graz, Austria in 1947 into a hard-working, working-class family Schwarzenegger's early life was marked by post-war austerity, discipline and competitiveness. The young Arnold responded positively to his upbringing, but it was the influence of America that seemed to loom large in his ambitions for the future.

His first body-building title – the 'Junior Mr Europe' – came in 1965, and began a decade in which he would win every trophy the sport had to offer, ultimately scooping an unprecedented thirteen world titles.

In 1968 Schwarzenegger moved to Los Angeles where he worked as a bricklayer, whilst being groomed for body-building success by the promoter Joe Weider, who was also responsible for arranging his protégé's first movie appearance in 1969. Apparently, with little understanding of what he was about Schwarzenegger took the lead in a comedy called *Hercules Goes Bananas* (later reissued under the name *Hercules in New York* in an attempt to make it sound like a more serious work). Further walk on roles were to follow, but his first real film breakthrough came with *Pumping Iron* (1977), which chronicled his real life attempt to take his sixth consecutive 'Mr Olympia' title.

The film was lauded by many critics, some of whom were impressed inevitably by his physical presence, 'Schwarzenegger lights up the film like neon every time he comes on stage ... he looks like a walking incarnation of the Mighty Thor' (*New York magazine*), whilst others, such as Richard Schickl of *Time*, were to identify other, sometimes more subtle characteristics, 'A cool, shrewd and boyish charmer, he exudes the easy confidence of a man who has always known he will be a star of some kind'. Film stardom of 'some kind' indeed followed, as for his first speaking role in *Stay Hungry* (1976) Schwarzenegger, playing opposite Jeff Bridges and

Sally Field, won an acting award: the Golden Globe for Most Promising Newcomer. Schwarzenegger played to type as a reigning 'Mr Austria' desperately trying to raise money to pay off a debt to a gym owner.

It was again to be the body that earned Schwarzenegger his next film advancement with his starring role in the Robert E. Howard inspired *Conan the Barbarian* (1981) and *Conan the Destroyer* (1984) as the eponymous sword and sorcery hero Conan. Both films were financial losers at the box office, but did enough to establish Schwarzenegger's ability to hold a lead role and to make him a feasible target for future action genre movies.

Thus it was that at one of Hollywood's endless rounds of parties Mike Medavoy, one of the cofounders of Orion Pictures, found himself convincing Schwarzenegger that he should take a look at the screenplay for *The Terminator*, with an eye to playing the lead, an heroic time-travelling warrior from the future who journeys back in time to ensure the survival of humanity.

Instead Schwarzenegger took on the role of the hero's arch enemy – the time-travelling cyborg from the future who journeys back in time to ensure the eventual enslavement and destruction of humanity. Schwarzenegger stole the show. The film was a success (see Contexts: Production History).

Schwarzenegger subsequently capitalised on this success with a spate of action films: *Commando* (1985); a return to sword and sorcery with *Red Sonja* (1985); *Raw Deal* (1986); *The Running Man* (1987); *Predator* (1987) and *Red Heat* (1988). He further attempted to broaden his range in several comedies, the most successful of which were *Twins* (1988) and *Kindergarten Cop* (1990), but it was his roles in the blockbuster hits *Total Recall* (1990) and *Terminator 2: Judgement Day* (1991) that finally cemented his stronghold on the expensive, special-effects-crammed action genre. *Terminator 2* reportedly costing over $80 million, a budget that included $14 million for Schwarzenegger, twice the entire budget for the original *Terminator*.

The early 1990s began to see a slide in action films and action heroes had to prove more adaptable. Schwarzenegger had already proved himself more than capable, having cast himself as the kinder, gentler protective cyborg in *Terminator 2*, but such moves were not without risks. *The Last*

biographies

Arnold Schwarzenegger
relaxes on set

a product of the American Dream

Action Hero (1993) marketed at a younger audience, and in which comedy and self-parody were as important as the violence, proved a large, expensive failure. Hollywood's confidence in Schwarzenegger was shaken.

It is very tempting to see Schwarzenegger's rise as a product of the American Dream: the latter day immigrant whose dedication and hard work sees him climbing the ladder of success and scaling the heights of fame and fortune, indeed it is almost impossible to regard such icons without resort to such clichéd idiom, after all it is through their experiences that such clichés are born.

There are, however, inevitably other factors, cultural and political, that play their part in such success:

> His path from Mr Universe to major Hollywood star was made possible by changes in the film industry: the rise of fantasy, science fiction, and action adventure genres after *Star Wars*, the return of heroism on a grand scale after a series of counter–cultural anti–heroes in the 1970s, and the importance of physical culture in the 1980s.
>
> *Hill and Gibson, 1998, p. 517*

JAMES CAMERON

In his 1997 biography of James Cameron, *Dreaming Aloud*, Christopher Heard cites the defining moment in Cameron's life as seeing Stanley Kubrick's *2001: A Space Odyssey*. 'I just couldn't figure out how all those visual effects were done, and I wanted badly to know, to understand what I was seeing. I went back to see the movie ten times trying to get inside it.'

The fifteen-year-old's reaction was to produce his own homemade 16mm versions of self-penned science fiction sagas in space. Trying to recreate the visions he had in his mind with limited equipment and a lack of technical knowledge served only to encourage the frustrated Cameron. Thus was born a technical interest in how film could create the most fantastic of visual effects that would serve to distinguish James Cameron's directional style, and twenty-nine years later would see him recreating the sinking of the Titanic in his multi-Oscar winning film of the same name.

THE TERMINATOR

biographies

He would, however, have to wait a further ten years after this initial inspirational encounter to seriously embark upon a career in film.

James Cameron was born in 1954 in the Canadian town of Kapuskasing, Ontario. Cameron's father was an electrical engineer who, like Gustav Schwarzenegger, was a strict disciplinarian, and his mother, an artist and homemaker. A further artistic influence upon the young Cameron was his grandmother, a schoolteacher, who instilled in him a love of literature. As a youth he was a born tinkerer, who displayed a natural hands-on curiosity about how things worked, and it is interesting to note how the two inherited impulses – a fascination for the technical and a love of story – have guided Cameron through his career. Even at college he found himself switching from physics to English literature, 'I didn't know if I wanted to be a scientist or an artist' (Heard, 1997, p. 8). By 1976 he had dropped out of college, married a local waitress and was earning what he could truck driving.

It was again to be a film that provided the next turning point in Cameron's life, for the summer of 1977 witnessed the release of the George Lucas film *Star Wars*. 'I was really upset when I saw Star Wars. That was the movie that I wanted to make. After seeing that movie I got really determined. I decided to get busy' (Heard, 1997, p. 8). He renewed his passion for home filming, always with the main intent of figuring out ways to create the visual effects he so enjoyed on screen.

Cameron's dream of being in the film industry finally became a reality in 1979, when he applied for the job of special effects camera man with Roger Corman's New World Pictures. The company had no need of camera men at the time, but Cameron accepted the more lowly position of miniature model maker, figuring, in true Hollywood tradition, that no matter where he started there would be plenty of opportunity to advance. Indeed, this is exactly what happened, with Cameron climbing several rungs even in the space of the first film he was to work on: *Battle Beyond the Stars* (1980).

Roger Corman, born in 1926, is widely recognised as one of the most successful American independent film makers of all time. In 1970 he set up his own company 'New World Pictures' and increasingly began to produce rather than direct his films. His vast output and approach to film making not only earned him financial success and cult critical status, but provided countless other film makers with the opportunity to learn the trade, and amongst those who began as overworked, lowly paid apprentices are the likes of Martin Scorsese, Jonathan Demme, Francis Coppola, Ron Howard, Joe Dante and actors the calibre of Jack Nicholson.

When Cameron joined New World most of these apprentices had gone on to make names for themselves working for the major studios but the Corman ethos was still the same: replicate the big budget blockbuster for a fraction of the price in a fraction of the time. The science fiction adventure story *Battle Beyond the Stars* saw Cameron move from miniature model builder to head of visual effects, a position further consolidated by Cameron's firing of the art director, and taking on the job himself, to gain overall control of the artistic and visual side of what was, at $2 million, the studio's most expensive film to date.

Cameron's ruthless, tunnel-visioned ambition made him few friends, but he got the job done and began to establish a reputation. In 1980 he was asked to produce special effects for another science fiction adventure movie *Escape from New York* by director John Carpenter, who had already made his mark in the low budget independent sector with *Dark Star* (1974), *Assault on Precinct 13* (1976) and, one of the most successful independent films ever made, *Halloween* (1978).

As with *Battle Beyond the Stars* Cameron showed himself totally adept at creating interesting and convincing visual special effects using a combination of technical understanding, artistic flair and practical problem solving. Carpenter was impressed: 'Jim Cameron's work just knocked me on my ass. I assigned him something I knew was impossible to do and he did it with a brilliant simplicity and dedication to achievement' (Heard, 1997, p. 24).

Further involvement in New World films followed, but Cameron was always itching to move on upwards, and after only two years he got the chance when Corman needed quickly to find a director for a low budget follow-up to Joe Dante's horror film *Piranha* (1978).

An Italian producer, Ovidio G. Assonitis, was responsible for the venture, and it was he who approached Corman after having trouble with the director he had originally chosen. A debut director was the target in order to keep costs low and to enable Assonitis to have full reign over the project. The movie, *Piranha 2: The Spawning* (1982), was fraught with difficulties from the offset: the badly organised crew spoke only Italian; under financing meant that there were no stunt men, so the actors were forced to do their own stunts – Lance Henriksen breaking his hand in the process; the costumes were so poor that the cast made do with their own clothes and what they could scrape together; and Cameron was so disappointed with the rubber piranha that he worked through the night creating his own. Cameron's job was further made virtually impossible by Assonitis, who refused to show him any of the dailies, telling him, 'it's shit, nothing cuts' and denying him any part in the editing process.

This is the point at which Cameron snapped and decided, famously, to take matters into his own hands. He broke into the editing room using a credit card, searched through the countless film cans until he found his film, taught himself to use their editing equipment, and returned night after night to piece the film together the way he wanted.

It was at this point, feeling 'pissed off and alienated', living broke and sick with flu in a hotel in Rome, that he awoke one night from a feverish dream with a vivid image of a robot-hitman coming from the future hell bent on destruction. Later he 'drew a sketch of half a terminator, which looked very much like the final one, crawling after a girl who was injured who couldn't get up and run. He had a kitchen knife and he pulled himself over the floor with it dragging his broken arm. I thought that was a really horrific image'.

The fate of *Piranha 2: The Spawning* is perhaps best summed up by Cameron himself, who looking back on the project, labelled it, 'the best flying piranha movie ever made'.

Cameron next applied himself to two screen-writing jobs, both sequels to successful projects, *Rambo: First Blood Part 2* and *Alien 2,* which would later become *Aliens.* He had also taken his nightmarish vision of a killer robot from the future and turned it into a screenplay that he thought had potential. *First Blood* (1982) had been a successful vehicle for action star

biographies background

and Schwarzenegger rival, Sylvester Stallone. The sequel was intended to take the original film's hero back to the fields and jungles of Vietnam in order to rescue comrades still held prisoner by the Viet Cong. Whilst Cameron's original script emphasised the 'psychological effect of being in Vietnam and the secondary trauma of coming back', the finished version bears more the mark of Stallone's handiwork. As Cameron explained to *The New York Times*, 'The action is mine: the politics are Stallone's. ... He took it a little further to the right than I would have, but that's fair. As in any collaborative effort, everybody sort of ... pees in the bucket.'

Following the success of *The Terminator*, Cameron's career has followed a steady pattern of success, his films, regardless of critical acclaim, have proved ever more popular at the box office and in subsequent video sales, accumulating in the process an array of Academy Awards, especially for their strong visual impact. *Aliens* (1986), co-scripted with Walter Hill and David Giler, won Academy Awards for Best Visual Effects and for Best Sound Effects, grossing over $180 million worldwide. It also saw Cameron named Director of the Year by The National Association of Theatre Owners. *The Abyss* (1989) received mixed reviews, and according to Hollywood legend, was a nightmare shoot, but won an Oscar for Best Visual Effects and grossed $110 million worldwide, making back its not inconsiderable budget, but not achieving the hoped for blockbuster status. *Terminator 2: Judgement Day* saw Cameron and Schwarzenegger together again. It became the first movie to go past the $100 million budget, and then took over $500 million in worldwide grosses. Ancillary revenues, including worldwide video, TV and merchandising, brought the total revenue close to $1 billion (US). Once again, a Cameron film won an Oscar for Best Visual Effects as well as for Make-up, Sound and Sound Effects Editing.

Terminator 2 was also notable in that it saw the emergence of Cameron's own production company Lightstorm Entertainment Inc., which acted as associate producers to Carolco Pictures. *True Lies* (1994) was Lightstorm Entertainment's first full film. It initially received mixed reviews and settled with a total domestic gross of $150 million, a not too impressive figure when balanced against a high budget of $125 million, however, the total worldwide box office gross was over $365 million.

Cameron first met Kathryn Bigelow in 1989 when visiting the set of her film *Blue Steel* in order to meet Jamie Lee Curtis, whom Cameron was lining up as the female lead in *True Lies*. Bigelow had already made quite a reputation as an action film director with her debut film *Loveless* (1983) and the vampire movie, *Near Dark* (1987). A relationship between the two directors followed with Bigelow and Cameron marrying in 1989. Cameron went on to co-write Bigelow's 1991 film *Point Break* and served as its Executive Producer. He also co-wrote her 1995 film *Strange Days*.

This period further saw Cameron build on his interests in visual effects and digital production with the setting up of his two high-tech firms: Digital Domain and Lightstorm Technologies. Throughout his career as director Cameron has continued to make use of the skills that had enabled him to rise to prominence at New World, namely his technological understanding, which was put to good use finding practical ways to overcome the problems of shooting the effects he visualised in his mind. His impressive list of achievements includes several firsts: dialogue recorded underwater (*The Abyss*); a computer-created being using the technique of morphing (*Terminator 2*) and a digital colour-correction system for effects (*True Lies*). Now Cameron had his own companies to reap the long-term financial benefits of his ideas and a full time staff to develop and use them further.

Cameron's crowning moment to date has to be his 1997 film *Titanic*. With the standard 'Cameron as megalomaniac on set' stories circulating alongside alleged health and safety violations, the film in production was being seen as a prospective *Heaven's Gate* (1980), with its spiralling out-of-control budget. Cameron went as far as giving up his director's salary and his share of the film's profits in order to complete the project. In doing so he produced the most successful film of all time. It remained number one at the US box-office for an astonishing fifteen weeks, and it is the only film to gross more than $20 million for ten consecutive weekends. It was the fastest film to gross $250 million and $300 million, and the only film ever to gross $400 million in its initial release. On 23 March 1998, *Titanic* received 11 Academy Awards including Best Picture and Best Director. A modest Cameron announced, 'I'm the king of the world'.

director as auteur

Film making is by nature a collaborative process – the length of film credits at the end of a film should leave us in no doubt about the number of people required to create the film we have just seen. Auteur theory proposes that a major film, although a collaborative activity (involving many people at various stages of pre-production, production and post-production) can be regarded as the work of a single individual in exactly the same sense as a novel or painting and in so doing attempts to convey a personal vision or message.

The theory of authorship was first expounded by François Truffaut in a polemical article in the French journal *Cahiers du Cinéma* in 1954, in which he openly criticised what he saw as being the almost mechanical trans-ferring of script on to screen to produce what was considered quality French cinema of good taste and high culture, in which the best film technique was one that is not seen. For Truffaut and his collaborators, in what we have come to know as the New Wave, style becomes independent of the story, the idea being to stamp the film maker's identity on the film, by making the spectator more aware of the medium they were watching. Their aim was to dazzle the spectator with the possibilities of the film-making process. Such was their reaction against the over importance of the script they often abandoned it altogether, favouring improvisation and spontaneity. It led to a position which was aesthetic in that it argued for the necessity of a personal vision or style in a director's film. Film makers who triumphed by this theory included Alfred Hitchcock, Howard Hawks, Orson Welles, Fritz Lang and John Ford.

The theory involved artistic standards, while paradoxically rescuing a large body of popular films which had been consigned to the cultural junk heap by critics and theorists alike; in particular, genre films – westerns, musicals, thrillers, gangster films – were now deemed worthy of academic interest. Chiefly it became a way of teaching film in a tradition which was essentially modelled on literary studies: a 'canon' of director's best works could be constructed and examined for worth, often along the lines of a consistent visual style, the composition and construction of a film in a particular way, or a regularly occurring theme.

director as auteur

Critics of auteur theory, including many directors, are quite right to be sceptical of such a theory, which has been made even more complex by shifting attitudes and definitions, however, it is always worthwhile applying even shifting criteria to a particular director in order to see if any patterns do indeed emerge.

The first most marked point is that, with the exception of his disastrous debut, every film directed by James Cameron has also been written by James Cameron, occasionally with the help of co-writers: Gale Anne Hurd is credited for work on *The Terminator*; producers Walter Hill and David Giler are credited on *Aliens*; and William Wisher shared the task of writing the screenplay of *Terminator 2*.

The original auteur theory suggests that the demands of the script are different to the demands of the workings of the author; the director should work against the script to impose his vision, but here we have a director whose script is the very transcript of that vision and Cameron's use of original vision is well documented. Two of his films are direct sequels: *Aliens* and *Terminator 2*: *True Lies* takes its inspiration from a French film *La Totale* and finds Cameron ready for a change of scene, after making four science fiction films in a row. *The Terminator* though, is born of an original vision. *The Abyss* is famously recorded as being inspired by a high school class trip to a science exhibition where Cameron first became acquainted with the experience of breathing liquid oxygen, which became the inspiration for his idea of an underwater race written about in a biology lesson. *Titanic* was apparently inspired by the first murky images on the news as the discovery of the wreck was reported on television – the subsequent historical romance was of Cameron's own making. Of the sequels, *Terminator 2* is obviously Cameron's vision, and although the original *Alien* provides Cameron with his main lead and protagonist, he clearly subjected it to his own vision, to the extent that producers Walter Hill and David Giler were so impressed with his initial screenplay that they suggested he might direct it himself.

Perhaps it is the 'spectacular' that serves to define Cameron's visual style. After all, as an action director he clearly prefers to work in a genre known for its high-intensity action set pieces. For Cameron it is not a matter of preferring a particular type of shot, it is more a case of trying to shoot the seemingly impossible so that it is as convincing as possible. Whether it be a nuclear holocaust, a nightmare future world ruled by machines, an underwater race of aliens, a colony of the most ferocious alien creatures known to man, a death defying rescue by Harrier jump jet on the painstaking reconstruction of a tragic disaster at sea, the particular shot will be aimed at carefully steering audience expectations and involvement, but it will count for nothing if the image is not believable. Indeed, Cameron's whole way of working seems geared towards controlling the set and everything that happens on it in order to get that final shot just right.

> Working with Jim Cameron is unique because he is basically every-thing! He writes the screenplay, he comes up with the concept, and he directs the scenes. He wants to do his own lighting and he wants to work the camera himself. He wants to do everything. You see him using the smoke machine and you see him putting on the blood and trying to do your makeup even though the makeup and special effects people have done it already. But he has to try and improve on it somehow. So he really has his fingers in every aspect of the movie. That is why a Jim Cameron movie has that look, that special, unique look.
>
> *Schwarzenegger in Heard, 1997, p. 71*

Cameron has a reputation as a fearsome, no-nonsense director who sets high standards and expects everyone around him to deliver them. On the set of *True Lies* he apparently forbade his crew to go to the toilet whilst on set, telling them that anyone who went to the bathroom could 'just keep walking'.

Whilst Cameron is primarily labelled as an action director, his films have moved through sub-genres of this category, taking in science fiction, espionage-cum-romantic comedy and historical romance. All have indeed proved highly spectacular action-filled movies with a composition and construction to match, but thematically too there are clear links between them. No matter how spectacular the wider world of the film Cameron seems drawn to the deeply personal level of his characters and their relationships. At the heart of *The Terminator* is a love story between Reese and Sarah Connor. It serves to develop the characters and forms a crucial prop for the whole plot. It is an idea that Cameron returns to again and again: at the outset of *The Abyss* Bud and Lindsay Brigman are estranged, but rediscover the depth of their affection for each other; in *True Lies* Schwarzenegger plays Harry Tasker, the James Bond type secret agent, who realises that he also needs to devote time to saving his marriage, as well as saving the world. For Jack and Rose in *Titanic* theirs is a love that overcomes barriers of class, even though it is doomed by that greatest of maritime disasters, the sinking in 1912 of the luxury liner.

Cameron's interest in relationships extends beyond notions of romantic love to a clear affection for family ties. In *Aliens* he deepens Ripley's character, not only is she the toughened survivor of the first film, she is now placed in a position of mother to the rescued child, Newt, and is allowed at least the potential for a close relationship with Corporal Hicks. In *Terminator 2* it is the role of father to the young John Connor that the reprogrammed T-800, Schwarzenegger again, finds itself occupying, much to the bemusement of mother Sarah Connor:

```
Watching John with the machine it was suddenly so
clear the terminator would never stop, it would
never leave him, and it would never hurt him, never
shout at him or get drunk and hit him, or say it
was too busy to spend time with him, it would
always be there and it would die to protect him.
Of all the would-be fathers who came and went over
the years this thing, this machine was the only one
who measured up. In an insane world it was the
sanest choice.
```

Within these relationships there emerge further constant patterns of characterisation. Cameron tends towards strong female characters, some of whom do not always realise their potential at first. Sarah Connor's journey from waitress to guerrilla freedom fighter is charted over the course of two of Cameron's films. The character of Ripley had already been established in Ridley Scott's *Alien* (1979) and there could be no doubting her resilience and toughness, but Cameron added depth to the character. Sigourney Weaver was nominated for an Academy Award for her reprisal of the role.

His male lead characters are not lessened by the strength of the female characters. If anything it makes them more interesting than their conventional action hero counterparts. They possess an emotional side quite distant from patriotic gung-ho heroism. It prompts their actions, and often leads ultimately to an act of self-sacrifice: Reese's last ditch attempt to destroy T-800; Bud Bigman's apparent self-sacrifice in running out of air, having successfully defused the nuclear warhead; the good T-800 being lowered at its own request, its job done, into the vat of molten metal that will consume it; Jack dying, freezing to death in the icy Atlantic waters knowing that he has done his best to save Rose.

Even with underlying themes there is a sense of continuation across Cameron's work: the ability of individuals to make a difference, especially when the powers that represent authority cannot be trusted to do so, concern over atomic war and the use and abuse of technology – all have their place in Cameron's oeuvre.

Within the course of an action film there may not always be the time to develop such themes fully, but their re-occurrence suggests they are issues that Cameron cares strongly about and wants to deal with in his works, even if they may sometimes be dismissed as 'pretentious' or a little formulaic by critics of action adventure films.

Finally, as critics have continued to argue for and against the merits of auteur theory, it is the industry itself that has adopted the idea as a means of marketing its product. Under the old studio system (see Contexts: Industrial) Hollywood was able to promote its films through the distinguishing studio identities, but the studio system declined and disappeared leaving a kind of vacuum, which director identity helped to fill. Thus we now have a preponderance of films prefaced by reference to the director's name *The Terminator* itself is prefaced by the wording:

director as auteur

Hemdale Presents

A Pacific Western Production

of A James Cameron Film

For the directors themselves the changing studio systems meant the loss of long-term contracts, where they worked for a studio to produce a certain number of films. Now they tend to be hired on a film-by-film basis. There is thus a need for directors to establish themselves through a handling of narrative and visual style in a distinctive and ultimately successful way in order to be considered for up and coming projects. So, whilst directors were once labelled auteurs as part of a debate about film theory, they now tend to set themselves up as auteurs in order to establish themselves. It has a certain absurdity, but auteur theory has become a kind of auteur practicality.

narrative & form

> Narrative is essentially a way of organising material. It consists of
> both the plot or story line used by the storyteller and the methods
> employed to tell that story.
>
> *Price, 1996, p. 33*

Narrative in film may be explained in a variety of ways. To begin with it may
be useful to identify what Price terms 'the methods' employed in the
creation of a story on screen, in which case we require an understanding
of the language of film – the grammar by which each visual segment
of that story is organised, arranged and presented to the viewer, and how
the viewer is meant to respond to and be involved in understanding that
story.

Secondly, as narrative is a universal activity central to how human beings
make sense of their experiences of life, through a range of means from
anecdote through to the most highly regarded literature, it is also useful to
explore the body of thinking that enables us to make sense of the
underlying theory behind it – its functions, rationale and significance.

film narrative

In *Film Art: An Introduction* David Bordwell begins the process of explaining
narrative language in film by making the distinction between story and
plot. He defines story as, 'all the events we see and hear, plus all those we
infer or assume to have occurred, arranged in their presumed causal
reactions, chronological order, duration, frequency and spatial locations. [It
is] Opposed to plot, which is the film's actual presentation of certain events
in the narrative'.

Applying this definition to *The Terminator* the opening premise of the film's
story may be summarised as follows:

We begin in the year 2029 in the aftermath of a nuclear war caused by an

film narrative

all powerful defence network computer, which was originally created to run all of the US systems, but using its own intelligence decided that humankind was the ultimate threat and should thus be exterminated. The survivors of this war were to be rounded up by automated factory-created machines for orderly disposal in concentration camps. However, there has emerged one man, John Connor, who has rallied the remaining humans and encouraged them to fight back. The humans are on the brink of winning the war against the machines, who see their only remaining course of action being to try to wipe from existence the guerrilla leader, John Connor. The chosen method is to send back in time a terminator: an infiltration unit designed to infiltrate and wipe out nests of guerrilla fighters. In order to infiltrate successfully the terminators must pass for human, so they have been designed part machine (a virtually indestructible micro-processor controlled skeleton with hydraulic muscles and tendons of flexible cable) and part man (a surface layer of living human tissue that behaves like normal human skin). The task of this particular terminator is to locate and kill John Connor's mother at a point in time before she has conceived her son, thus with her death the guerrilla leader will never exist. The time displacement equipment will only allow living tissue to journey through time, so unclothed and unarmed the terminator journeys back to complete his mission (the outer layer of skin presumably masking the metal beneath). As past records have been badly damaged the only information the terminator has to go on is the name of its target and the city she lives in.

John Connor, having discovered the plan to kill his mother and having gained access to the time displacement equipment decides that a human guerrilla fighter must also make the journey back in time in order to protect her. Kyle Reese, a sergeant in Tech. Comm. volunteers for this mission. Close to John Connor, he has an advantage over the terminator in that he knows what Sarah Connor looks like. He has developed a strong affection for Sarah through listening to tales of her life and being in possession of a photograph of her taken sometime around the mid 1980s. He believes that once he has been transported the time machine will be destroyed.

Upon arriving in present day (1984) Los Angeles the two time travellers separately begin tracking down Sarah Connor: one to kill her, the other to save her ...

This story line is broadly speaking a linear and chronological account of events that follow a clear succession of cause and effect.

This is, however, not what we are presented with on screen:

After the initial credit announcing a James Cameron film we see a blackened screen and hear an eerie wind that gives way to the sound of explosions and what may be laser fire. A caption reading 'Los Angeles 2029 AD' appears over a desolate ruined landscape. We hear the futuristic craft before we see it, but its intention is clear, it is searching the ruins and firing laser fire at whatever is its target. We hear the steady rumble of a tank and then see its tracks rolling over a road of human skulls. We get a fleeting glimpse of human fighters running amidst the ruins. They are clearly the targets of the machines. A shot of the skulls foregrounded, whilst in the background the giant futuristic machines roam, concludes this scene.

An introductory text appears:

```
The machines rose from the ashes of the nuclear
fire.
Their war to exterminate mankind had raged for
decades, but the final battle would not be fought in
the future.
It would be fought here, in our present.
Tonight ...
```

The opening credits follow.

The next scene, the post-credit scene, like that of the opening, leads with a caption, this time 'LA 1984 1.52 am' and we see a refuse lorry lifting garbage in the early hours. Its engine suddenly cuts out, much to the surprise of its human operator. Suddenly the surrounding environment seems caught in a lightning storm of sorts. The lorry driver makes a run for it and we observe a naked figure crouching in a statuesque pose, as a mist dissipates around him. The figure stands and appears to take in his surroundings, below him lies night-time LA.

The figure, who seems undaunted by his naked state, encounters three punks, who seek to have some fun at his expense. The naked man demands their clothes, and when met with hostility he throws two of the punks aside and pulls the heart from the third. The one conscious punk hurriedly undresses.

Another shot of the city street at night introduces the third scene as we witness the arrival of the second naked man in similar conditions to the first, although this man and the manner of his arrival are strikingly different to what we have previously seen with the first man.

This second man likewise attempts to clothe himself, taking the pants from a tramp and helping himself to sneakers and a trench coat from a department store into which he had fled to escape the attentions of the chasing police force. This man, like the first, has spoken few words, stopping only to demand the date from one of the chasing police officers. Much to the officer's bewilderment it is actually the date in terms of the year that the man wants to know ...

The difference between story and plot is readily apparent. Following a linear pattern of cause and effect the story makes absolute sense, in as much as we are to suspend our disbelief and accept this notion of a present that can involve time travel and world domineering machines. We accept the pattern of events and can understand why each action is taken and that each effect is the consequence of a previous cause. In plot, however, there are gaps in our understanding. The audience is deliberately not given the entire picture.

Rather like in certain detective narratives we are introduced to an effect (a naked man appearing from nowhere) but not the causes (why he suddenly appears, where he has come from). By suppressing causes in this way film creates mystery and intrigue.

It is clearly Cameron's intention to make his audience work – to mystify us somewhat so that we are forced to ask questions thus deepening our involvement with the events on screen, as well as confronting us with a succession of highly dramatic spectacles from the violent confrontation with the punks to the cat and mouse chase through the darkened alleyways of LA.

CAUSE AND EFFECT AND INFERENCE

Narrative development depends upon the way in which cause–effect logic is worked out by the audience, through their ability to identify the events depicted in the scenes and link them. The role of storyteller/director is to create a pattern of cause and effect that is accessible, but also to manipulate the audience by playing with that pattern. At the beginning of the film Cameron has presented effects, but deliberately withheld the cause: we have the sudden arrival of the two naked men, but we have no concrete information about who they are or what they are about. We may infer from the opening futuristic scene and the manner of their arrival that they are something to do with this future war and the final battle that is referred to, but their exact reason for being transported back in time, if that is what has happened, is unknown. However, bit by bit we begin to piece together information about them: their manner of arrival has slight differences – one arriving composed, apparently unaffected by his journey, the other hits the pavement with a bang, almost appearing to be dropped there, his posture and expression suggesting discomfort and pain, his body, like the first, displaying athletic toning – although the first possesses a physique that is almost superhuman – but this second traveller is scarred and ill at ease with his nude state. The first traveller takes what he wants by force of the most brutal uncompromising kind. The second traveller takes what he needs, but causes no actual bodily harm. The two men thus share similarities, but are markedly different. Is their mission therefore the same, or are they here for different reasons? What, if anything, is their connection to the final battle?

Inference works not only with character. The onscreen information tells us that the first traveller arrives in LA in the year 1984 at 1.52 a.m. (no day or month is given). We are left to infer that the second traveller arrives in the same place at pretty much the same time. Several clues are given that enable such inference. No further onscreen information is given for the second traveller, so we are to understand that this information should serve for both scenes. In both it is clearly night time. The police officers chasing the second traveller are clearly identifiable as belonging to the LAPD – their cars being clearly marked. Furthermore, there is continuity between the two scenes that suggest they are parallel developments. As the first man prepares to dress in the clothes of the punks a siren is heard as if in response to his crime of killing; this siren is then seen as belonging to a speeding police car that runs through the first shot of the next scene in which we see the arrival of the second traveller.

FLASHBACK

Another narrative technique often employed to develop character is the use of flashback and James Cameron employs this twice during the film. Use of flashback involves rearranging narrative events in a non-linear order and is commonly seen as a method of upsetting a film's cause and effect. Here it has the added dimension of being a flashback into events that a character has experienced within his own time frame, but that exist in the future, hence Cameron's term 'future flashbacks'.

The first such scene occurs as the second time traveller steals a car from outside a construction yard. The heavy earth moving machinery reminds the traveller of the machines of destruction in the future against which he, a guerrilla fighter, attempts to do battle. Is he then a representative of mankind? Indeed the manner of his arrival would suggest that he has the vulnerability of a human, and, perhaps as further proof, he has, as yet, taken no action to harm anyone.

The film's plot continues in this vein throughout its opening phase. Next we are given clues as to the mission of the second man. In a phone booth he uses the directory to locate a Sarah Connor. Soon we will see the first traveller go through the same process, only to begin executing the first of three such names as they are listed in the directory. In the meantime we have been introduced to a Sarah Connor, waitress at a burger restaurant, who would seem to be as remote from the two time travellers as you could possibly get.

film narrative

PARALLELISM

A further technique of narration is revealed here, as Cameron appears to be telling three stories at once – in separate scenes that will eventually merge into one clear plot he follows the experience of the first traveller, the second traveller and Sarah Connor. He opens up a further strand by introducing two police detectives: Traxler and Vukovich, who have been assigned the job of dealing with the murders of victims named Sarah Connor. Parallelism is the technique whereby two or more separate actions unfold on the screen side by side through alternating sequencing of events, and Cameron exploits it to full potential, enabling his plot once established to unfold at a very fast rate indeed. One further advantage to this technique is, as we have already noted, to permit a parallel interpretation of character – similarities and differences between leading characters are made quite clear, thereby aiding the audience in the process of inference.

ELLIPSIS

Having firmly established a fast pace to the momentum of the narrative Cameron takes further steps to accelerate that drive. The next technique he employs is that of ellipsis; shortening the unfolding of plot by missing out the second Sarah Connor murder. He has already established the first time traveller as a killer whose target is the three Sarah Connors in the phone directory. We have observed his murder of the first Sarah, and we know that we are following the story of another Sarah. As we begin to worry for the safety of 'our' Sarah, we suddenly learn through the police detectives of the murder of the second Sarah Connor – Cameron has saved film time, moved the plot further forward and increased the anxiety of the audience by not showing something.

EXPLANATION AND REVELATION

Within any complex narrative there emerges a moment when inference is not enough and explanation is required to knot the various strands together. The timing and handling of such a moment is obviously crucial to the audience's ability to follow and enjoy the plot. Cameron delays the moment for as long as possible – the second Sarah Connor has been

30 THE TERMINATOR

The terminator (Arnold Schwarzenegger)
aims to complete its mission by killing
Sarah Connor (Linda Hamilton) in the
Tech Noir nightclub

executed, the police are desperate to contact the third and last Sarah Connor; the two time travellers are fully armed and the first charged with the task of carrying out the executions, is clearly well up to the task, having killed at least six times without compunction. The motives of the second still remain something of a mystery – he has stalked Sarah Connor but taken no direct action – whilst the third Sarah Connor, beginning to realise her life is in some kind of danger, desperately attempts to contact someone who can make a difference – the police or her flatmate Ginger. The strands of the first phase come together in the Tech Noir nightclub – Sarah finally manages to make contact with the police, who promise to be there any second; the first time traveller, executioner and no doubt the terminator of the film's title makes his move on the third Sarah Connor, the second traveller plays his hand and steps in to defend Sarah against attack. A spectacular set-piece gunfight is followed by the first of several car chases, and it is now, whilst the action drives the film and the audience has seen the merging of the parallel plots that Cameron allows the first moment of revelation and explanation to unfold. The time travellers are given names and roles, the plot is given its cause and effect explanation and the audience, satisfied with the affirmation of all that has been correctly inferred, prepares itself for events to come. What is perhaps most remarkable about this unfolding of explanation is that it begins during what is already an exciting and action-packed moment. The chase, begun on foot through darkened alleyways, has moved on to the highway – the terminator is in hot pursuit of Sarah and Reese, whilst the LAPD chase both of them. In the Tech Noir Reese announced himself to Sarah with a dramatic, 'Come with me if you want to live'. The dialogue in the car is no less intense. Reese barks explanations in a military voice seemingly used to giving orders and with a sense of no nonsense urgency. 'Do exactly what I say. Exactly. Don't move unless I say. Don't make a sound unless I say. Do you understand?'

He introduces himself, explains his role as time-travelling protector, and explains the make up and friction of the terminator, leaving a stunned Sarah in no doubt at all about her position, 'Listen. Understand. That Terminator is out there. It can't be reasoned with, it can't be bargained with ... it doesn't feel pity or remorse or fear ... and it absolutely will not stop.

Ever. Until you are dead'. The explanation continues when Reese pulls into an underground car park, where Cameron has Reese reveal the final piece in the narrative jigsaw. Sarah's importance to Reese, and her reason for being the terminator's target: she is to be mother to the future saviour of mankind. A bombshell of a revelation, but even here there is no time to dwell on details. The tension of the chase has been maintained throughout the scene as police patrol cars continue to circulate the underground car park, and we see shots of the terminator, who, as we are told, clearly will not give up the chase. Suddenly Reese and Sarah are spotted and, once again, the terminator is on their trail.

Once established, the plot follows this pattern of narrative through, incorporating further parallelism, flashback, ellipsis and moments of explanation/revelation, but Cameron is inventive and eager to explore the potential of these conventions, as well as maintaining that forward drive and the interests of his audience.

The second moment of explanation occurs, again under very tense circumstances, when Reese is questioned by the criminal psychologist, Silberman, inside the police station. Here we learn more about the future war and how Reese travelled through time, but all this falls on ears unwilling or unable to believe. Sarah is being cocooned in the seemingly rational explanation of the police; Reese is 'a loon'; the attacker in the Tech Noir must have been wearing body armour. The significance for the audience is the dramatic irony of the situation, whilst Reese screams over the video tape, 'You still don't get it. He'll find her. That's what he does. All he does ... you can't stop him. He'll wade through you ... Reach down her throat, and pull her fucking heart out...'. The audience knows that he speaks the truth, and an even more confused Sarah is anything but safe.

The third and final moment of explanation occurs through flashback at a point in the film, where there is a marked contrast to everything that has gone before. Having escaped from the carnage of the police station Sarah and Reese abandon their car and spend the night in a drainage culvert that passes under the road. The audience at last has a chance to draw breath. The characters are exhausted; Sarah has an opportunity to question Reese, although it is more from a point of accepting what he has to say rather than disbelieving him, and Reese has wounds to tend. As they huddle closer Sarah asks Reese to tell her more about the future and Reese begins his account of life as a guerrilla fighter. The scene in future flashback moves to the underground shelters in which the remnants of humanity barely survive. Suddenly this picture is interrupted as a terminator infiltrates the underground hideout and begins to fulfil its deadly task. The next shot that returns us to the present world of Sarah and Reese is significant, because we see Sarah suddenly wake from a nightmare in which she was clearly dreaming about Reese's world, 'Your world ... it's pretty terrifying'. What began as Reese's narrative ends as Sarah's dream. A bond has been forged and strengthened between the two characters, between the present and the future, between what is being done and what has to be done. Significantly, as the two leave the shelter of the culvert night has turned to day and there is a moment of calm before their journey continues.

At this point also Cameron opens up a neat pattern of circulatory by allowing the viewer to see Reese in his moment of future flashback holding a worn, torn photograph of Sarah. As the terminator opens fire Reese loses the photograph and we watch it burn in the flames. Strangely neither Reese nor Sarah mention this photograph, until later in the motel room when Reese attempts to explain his feelings for Sarah, 'John Connor gave me a picture of you once. I never knew why. It was very old. Torn. Faded. You were young like you are now. You weren't smiling ... just a little sad ... I always wondered what you were thinking at that second'.

The photograph served the plot in that it enabled Reese to identify Sarah – his one advantage over the terminator, but it further adds to the story line in the epilogue, when we see the original photograph being taken by a Mexican boy at a gas station as Sarah sits in contemplation of all that happened and all that is to come, leaving the audience with shots of thunder clouds over the Mexican desert and the news that 'there is a storm coming in'.

Towards the end of the film Cameron has one more narrative trick up his sleeve:

narrative

> Cameron is very aware of what he calls the 'recency effect', that the most recent thing an audience sees is what sticks in their mind. Because of that, Cameron scripts often make use of the double climax, and *The Terminator* is no exception.
>
> *Bernardin, 1995, p. 51*

The false ending is yet another play on cause and effect; but only partially showing an effect or by delaying if a sudden revelation is possible or even a twist upon our expectation.

The terminator seems to be closing in. Another high intensity car/motorbike chase has left Sarah and Reese on foot, having only just escaped from their upturned pick-up truck, which has been rammed by the terminator in his hijacked gasoline tanker truck. Sarah and Reese split up, but the terminator's tanker truck is bearing down on Sarah. Reese takes a homemade pipe bomb, inserts it at the rear of the tanker and dives for cover. The tanker explodes spectacularly. We see the terminator stumble from a blazing cab. It falls to the floor and lies still as its skin burns to a crisp. A figure emerges from the flames. It is Reese. The lovers embrace.

It seems like an ending, but behind the embracing lovers another figure rises up from the flames – the chrome plated skeleton that is the terminator minus skin. The chase is still on.

Reese and Sarah flee inside a building, which turns out to be an automated factory. Having fought hand to hand Reese plants his final pipe bomb amongst the hydraulic rods and cables of the terminator's skeleton. The explosion scatters the terminator's body parts throughout the factory. Amidst these scraps of metal a wounded Sarah finds the body of Reese. Again, we appear to have reached the end of the film, but as Sarah is trying to take in the loss of her lover, the skeleton rises again – this time the torso of the skeleton is able to pull itself along by its hands. Sarah crawls – the wound to her leg preventing her from walking – the terminator follows. The momentous battle between hunter and victim finally concludes as the terminator reaches out a hand to strangle Sarah and she presses the start button on the hydraulic press that crushes the 'life' out of the cyborg.

narrative may oscillate

POINT OF VIEW

Whilst narrative is, as Stuart Price defines, 'essentially a way of organising material' – the story that is told and how that story is organised in terms of plot – there are other elements that require consideration into how that narrative functions. Sound, whether real to the world of the film or added to it, as, for example, a soundtrack, not only creates atmosphere and tension, but also serves to manipulate the audience in their understanding of what is happening. In fact, all elements in what we shall term mise-en-scène (camera angle, lighting, costume...) serve to aid the audience in their understanding of what they see. These elements will be dealt with in the next section on 'Style', but one of the very significant factors in terms of how material is organised and presented to the viewer is point of view. Any discussion of point of view inevitably requires discussion of whose point of view we actually share, hence we must examine character.

character

The writer of a story has a choice about who tells that story; whether it be a character within the story line, in which case the writer opts for the intimate but tied first person; or the omniscient third person of an apparently uninvolved storyteller. There is even a third choice; the reader as character using the distinctly unnerving and quite rare second person.

The film director/screenplay writer is faced with similar choices. Restricted narration ties the representation of film narrative to one particular character only – the equivalent of first person. Omniscient narration allows the camera to roam freely taking up a seemingly neutral position. Writers of novels and short stories tend to opt very definitely for one or the other choices available, although there are many successful attempts to mix and blend styles. Most often in film though the narrative oscillates between the two, and whilst we may not always get to see a consistent view inside a character's mind – a monologue to camera or voiceover being the closest we get – we often have narratives that operate from several points of view.

This is indeed what we have with *The Terminator*. Whilst overwhelmingly omniscient the camera also makes interesting use of restricted narration.

character

Most notably perhaps is the involvement of the three main characters in sharing their point of view with the audience. In the earlier stages of the film when we share a character's point of view it is more often than not that of the terminator, whilst in the later stages, as she assumes a greater sense of responsibility, it is Sarah's point of view that predominates. Reese has his share of point of view shots throughout the whole film, but interestingly, especially as he is meant to occupy the role of hero, his point of view does not dominate any section. Sometimes these point of view shots are oblique in that point of view is suggested, whist at other times it is definitely intended. The function of these point of view shots are many and varied: they are useful in developing the plot – as Reese and the terminator scan the phone directory we see them locate the three Sarah Connors; they heighten the suspense of action scenes, such as the chase; and they serve to explain and symbolise relationships, such as in the love scenes between Reese and Sarah. It is the terminator's point of view shots, however, that gain an extra dimension as Cameron sometimes opts for an infra red computerised vision, which has data scrolling across the screen. Thus the terminator is provided with a unique way of seeing that confirms his alienness – his machine-like being.

The whole process of cause-effect logic upon which narrative development depends requires always an initial motivation; somebody does something, that is a cause, and an effect follows. This process, of course, requires a motivation, and that motivation is a character in the film.

THE TERMINATOR

The very title of the film gives prominence to the character of the terminator. He is the first traveller to arrive in the Los Angeles of 1984, and the first traveller to which we can ascribe a clear motive. Thus he is the first instigator of cause and effect; he is the initial provider of motivation. Even before the film has started this is the character that the audience has come to see – he is played by the star, whose image has been used to promote the film through advertising. His face is the main image on the posters that adorn the theatre foyer and as a result he is most readily associated with the film's title. The audience enters with the question 'What is a terminator?'.

Of course, the audience is a varied body – people enter the theatre knowing different things and with a range of expectations. Many of those coming to see *The Terminator* would be there because word of mouth (see Contexts: Production History) had informed them that it was worth seeing. Some might never have heard of Arnold Schwarzenegger; others would know him for his body-building and/or his role as Conan. Most, of those who had heard of him, would know that here was an actor not renowned for his acting abilities but possession of an impressive physical presence. It is that presence that Cameron first reminds us of in such a startling manner, that even at the end of the film when the terminator is stripped of every vestige of Schwarzenegger, it is still Arnold as machine skeleton that we see. Furthermore, character and star actor become so interlinked in this film that Schwarzenegger will always carry the tag of terminator, even some fifteen years later as he promotes his latest film, it is still the terminator label that journalists reach for.

When we first see the terminator it is Schwarzenegger the body-builder performing on stage. As the mist clears around the forecourt of the Griffith Park Observatory the camera pans from the fleeing dump truck driver to a kneeling gleaming naked body. The strength of that heavily muscular body cannot be doubted. It is emphasised by the low camera angle that forces its audience to look up across the solid blocks of pectorals to the impassive face beyond. Throughout, Schwarzenegger's body and face are lit from behind and the side, but they lack fill from the front. The ensuing shadows emphasise the bulk and the fact that it is sculpted; this is a strength that is made and intended. A close-up of Schwarzenegger's face emphasises the lack of expression (this isn't exactly acting, it's looking with style) and, as if in submission, the camera holds still whilst this impassive stare moves slowly from one side to the other taking everything in. The sculpted body then moves assuredly forward – obediently tracked by the camera to create an establishing shot that takes in the lights of night-time LA. Even the city seems somehow dwarfed by this powerful figure that is made all the more arrogant by its nakedness.

The shots that follow are very similar in establishing the commandeering strength of the character, his assuredness and determination to carry out a task to completion, but along with this they reveal a character who has the ability to kill without compunction whenever necessary. His first victims are the punks: as they pull out switch blades he brushes them aside, using his bare fist to puncture his main victim's ribcage, in the process hoisting the punk off the ground before allowing him to fall back to earth – the punk's now detached heart firmly in the terminator's grasp. The audience reaction to this killing may vary. It is clearly intended to be shocking but also exciting; we knew the naked man had strength but this act seems to go beyond strength – can human beings kill this way or is there something more superhuman to this figure? The punks themselves are perhaps easy targets – they will not easily engage audience sympathies – if at all. Their characters are quickly defined as drunken vandals lacking even basic respect for each other. It was they who sought 'fun' at the stranger's expense. It was they who were armed and were prepared to use the threat of their knives from the outset. This death is quickly followed by others: the shooting of the gun store owner; the execution of the first Sarah Connor; the reported execution of the second Sarah Connor; Matt, the boyfriend of Sarah's flatmate, Ginger and Ginger herself; innocent bystanders caught in the Tech Noir shootout; police officers charged with defending Sarah Connor; Sarah Connor's mother and finally, Sarah Connor's lover, Kyle Reese. A final body count of twenty-seven people.

Even when he is not killing he is symbolised as a destructive force: as his car pulls up outside the first Sarah Connor's house its wheels crush a child's toy truck – a neat foreshadowing of the destruction of the truck at the end of the film, and, as he steps across the floor of Sarah's apartment, he unknowingly crushes Ginger's headphones just as he has crushed the life out of Ginger herself.

A heartless killer who will stop at nothing, the terminator displays impeccable credentials as the film's villain, and thus should be justifiably feared, or at least roundly booed and hissed, during his every screen appearance. For Robert McKee there is a further edge to the character:

> Schwarzenegger's performance is perfect, but what makes that performance work is the writing which came up with a brilliant notion of contradiction between machine and human because this character is so utterly unpredictable. ... because he's machine and

human, that contradiction constantly keeps the audience in a state of awe, you can never be comfortable. In one scene he takes his eyeball out of his head to prepare himself and then combs his hair, and that's a piece of genius, it's seemingly simply but is a marvellous idea ... now the monster's all the more terrifying, for thanks to these moments we have no idea of what to expect from him, and therefore imagine the worst.

McKeen, 1993, p. 113

Others, such as Sean French, recognise a different kind of ambivalence in the character, mainly emanating from the star himself:

Cameron resists adding any humanising touches to the terminator. Schwarzenegger himself observed in *Interview* not entirely with approval, that there was some indirect humour, but it wasn't written for that; that was just the reaction of people. The audience response to the film revealed that there was something intrinsically attractive and comic about Schwarzenegger, even in the grimmest of contexts. The murder of Ginger ... is thoroughly in the genre of those slasher movies in which sexually active women are butchered one by one as some sort of psychopathic puritan revenge ... But because it was Arnie, audiences half knew that it was all in fun.

French,1996, p. 38

Dialogue often offers the greatest insight into how an audience is to react towards a character and how that character should be read. The character of the terminator, however, would appear to offer very little, having a mere eighteen lines of dialogue, a grand total of just seventy-four words. Most of these lines are purely functional, consisting of instructions and commands. Towards the end of the film, however, there are lines that hint at something more. Having enquired about Sarah Connor at the desk of the police station the terminator, now attired in shades and a motorbike jacket, leaves with the words: 'I'll be back'. There is a long effective pause while we wait for something to happen, and then the terminator's car crashes

the terminator has eighteen lines of dialogue

The terminator performs autosurgery

something intrinsically attractive and comic

The relentless fighting machine, that
is the terminator, takes on the LAPD

straight through the doorway announcing the terminator's entrance and his statement of intent. The famous 'I'll be back' line could be the terminator's way of closing the conversation or it could be an impassive matter of fact way of announcing what he was about to do, or it could serve as a hint of comic irony on the part of the terminator himself, just as it does for Cameron, the script writer. Likewise, when the terminator's state of hygiene is questioned by a cleaner at his hotel, we see through the terminator's point of view that he has a choice of replies. He opts for 'Fuck you asshole'. An effective choice as it gets rid of the cleaner, and for Cameron a reply that will tickle his audience, but also one of McKee's humanising moments.

What is clear is that the character of the terminator is more than just a villain. Yes, we root for Sarah and Reese as they attempt to flee the terminator's clutches, and there is surely welcome relief at the end of the film when the terminator is finally defeated, ironically, with the use of another machine. But audiences respond to the character in an almost unexpected way. As Cameron has it:

> In this film, you have it both ways. You root for Reese and Sarah, you want them to live, you feel the emotions. At the same time, you love to root for the bad guy; you want to see him get up again, you want to see him dumbfound the poor cops. There is a little bit of the terminator in everybody. In our private fantasy world we'd all like to be able to walk in and shoot somebody we don't like, or to kick a door in instead of unlocking it; to be immune, and just to have our own way every minute. The terminator is the ultimate rude person. He operates completely outside all the built-in social constraints. It's a dark, cathartic fantasy. That's why people don't cringe in terror from the terminator but go with him. They want to be him for that one moment.
>
> *Chute, 1985, p. 54*

REESE

The character of Reese gets to occupy the traditional role of hero – the romantic lead whose job it is to save the day and win the heart of the female lead – but as we have already seen the film already has a villain who is more than a villain, so what of its hero?

It is a feature of Cameron's use of parallelism to create contrast between the two time travellers. Much of Reese's early involvement in the film would appear to highlight this. He arrives second to the terminator and thus we compare the manner of his arrival with that of the first traveller. His actions to an extent follow those of the terminator, but, whereas the terminator's quest quickly becomes apparent, Reese's reasons for being are deliberately kept from us.

Whilst the terminator's arrival is one of almost studied poise and assuredness, Reese is dropped to ground as if from a considerable height. He is clearly muscular but is also physically scarred. His whole demeanour suggests discomfort, with his nakedness, the rigours of his journey and the environment in which he finds himself. As the terminator has done before him, Reese begins equipping himself: first with clothes and then a weapon. Again, the unfolding alternating stories reveal a series of contrasts: Reese robs a tramp of his trousers and takes an overcoat and a pair of sneakers from a department store, the rifle is stolen from an unmanned police car. No deaths have occurred at Reese's hands, whilst under similar circumstances the terminator has already killed, at least twice. The finished product bears further comparison: the terminator's attire, taken from the punks, suggests aggression – biker boots, combat trousers, studded fingerless gloves, and combat jacket replete with heavy duty bike chain; Reese, in contrast, sports the tramp's pants, an overcoat and a pair of Nike trainers. Whilst the terminator will stand out, Reese is more likely to blend in and there is a certain likeness to Reese's attire that suggests an ability to keep ahead during the chase and to tread carefully and quietly as necessity demands.

In terms of weapons also the contrast is pronounced. The terminator has armed himself with the most sophisticated and up-to-date hand guns and assault rifles for maximum efficiency; Reese makes do with a stolen police rifle, which he shortens for ease of use and concealment.

Throughout these early scenes, indeed it could be said of the whole film, the terminator is all forward momentum and action, Reese, however, takes

Michael Biehn as Kyle Reese

character

to the shadows. He seems to stalk Sarah Connor – trailing her and watching from a distance. When he finally makes his move it is to fulfil his first obligation as hero and defend Sarah from the terminator's attack in the Tech Noir.

In the ensuing chase it falls to him to explain everything and he does so with a military style efficiency that confirms what we have already seen in future flashback of Reese as a guerrilla fighter:

```
Do exactly what I say. Exactly. Don't move unless I
say. Don't make a sound unless I say. Do you
understand? ... I'm here to help you. Reese,
Sergeant/Tech-Com, DN38416 ... Assigned to protect
you. You've been targeted for termination.
```

His explanations are by necessity clipped and excited. He clearly has great admiration for the leader, who has sent him on his mission, and for the legend, that is Sarah Connor, the leader's mother. He bravely rescues Sarah from the Tech Noir attack and from the mayhem of the police station, but there is a vulnerability here that marks Kyle Reese a different type of hero than we may often be used to in the action adventure genre. Even in his explanation to Sarah there is a sense of insecurity, and this from the man who has been assigned to protect her. Whilst pretty certain about the terminator's ability, 'and it absolutely will not stop. Ever. Until you are dead', he is less certain about his own:

```
Sarah
      Can you stop it?
Reese
      Maybe with these weapons ... I don't know.
```

There is even an occasion when he attempts to talk tough as though he were the machine and not the terminator:

```
Reese
      Pain can be controlled. You disconnect it.
```

character

```
Sarah

      And so you feel nothing.

Reese

      It's better that way.
```

but this is the character that we saw arrive in discomfort, and put beside the terminator's total nonchalance (we have seen it repairing itself by removing an eye!) it has a brave but hollow ring.

It is also Sarah who prevents Reese from leaping out of their car guns blazing, when it is clearly apparent that the police heavily outnumber them, and that for the meantime the chase is up.

For a soldier, like Reese, born of war and knowing only war, it may come as no surprise to the viewer, that feelings such as love are often the hardest to come to terms with. Certainly Reese's admission of love is a stumbling and awkward affair, that finds Sarah once again picking up the pieces and leading him in their lovemaking.

There is further the sense of Reese as unwitting pawn. His known mission being to protect Sarah Connor, his unknown role being to father John Connor, as is hinted at in the epilogue in which Sarah decides to reveal her lover's identity to her son: 'Should I tell you about your father? That's a tough one. Will it change your decision to send him here ... knowing? ... I suppose I'll tell you ... I owe him that. And maybe it'll be enough if you know that in the few hours we had together we loved a lifetime's worth.'

For some, like Sean French, these vulnerabilities make for an unconvincing hero: instead of staying contemptuously silent in the face of police questioning Reese blabs away 'like a stoolie'; his explanations at times amounting to bleating about his own heroism; the scenes when he should engage our sympathies by revealing his emotions 'actually made him seem weak and neurotic'; and ultimately he fails in his duty as hero, by dying, and in so doing leaving the heroine to face the villain alone.

French's interpretation may seem harsh, but it is actually difficult to find anything at all upbeat about Reese as a hero. His vision is unremittingly bleak, and Cameron seems to deliberately exclude him from any of the film's dark humour. There are no wise-cracks for this action hero. Even his point of view shots are limited.

For others though, like Lillian Necakov, Reese's vulnerability is a welcome change, a mark of something new – a challenge to the Hollywood orthodoxy, and it is those parallels that support the reading: 'The parallels, in fact, have two major functions: a) to show that the Terminator is in fact, a product that man himself has created in man's own macho image, and b) to set Reese apart and to show that man need not fill that stereotypical role.'

Perhaps, Reese's role is ultimately to provide opportunities. Whilst we have a villain who is more than a villain, we now have a hero who is less than a hero, freeing the space for the final character of the triumvirate, Sarah Connor.

SARAH CONNOR

Sarah too is part of this parallelism. Her story is essential to that of the plot for unknowingly in the early sections she is to occupy the role of mother to the future saviour of mankind, and is thus the ultimate motivator of cause-effect as the target for termination and the subject for protection.

We know her name before we see her – her clocking-in card confirming what we already suspect, that this is the Sarah Connor who will occupy our interests. She first appears riding a motor scooter through the LA traffic on her way to work. There is an immediate contrast to the preceding scenes that have followed the arrival of the terminator and Reese. Sarah's opening scene is in daylight accompanied by a recognisably 'humanistic' score on piano. There is a degree of independence about the character: making her way to work, parking her motor scooter and patting the fibreglass mascot of her work place, Big Bob's family restaurant, 'Watch this for me, big buns'; but there is also a sense of the conventional: the neatly permed hair and the taste for soft pastel colours remind us that Sarah is no rebel. Her job as waitress leaves her frazzled and at the mercy of an impatient, unforgiving public. There is humour here, but it is often at her expense.

This juxtaposition of conventional and unconventional continues away from work in her personal life. In her shared apartment she and Ginger, her flatmate, prepare themselves for the evening ahead. Ginger is initially seen as vivacious, full of movement and life. Sarah dresses conservatively, Ginger undoing her top buttons for her as though to loosen her up. Sarah, this time at the mercy of her Porsche-driving date, is stood up. She consoles herself with inane dialogue to her pet lizard, Pugsley: 'You still love me, don't you Pugsley?' but this does not mean the end of her evening. Unafraid of venturing out alone she goes out to watch a movie.

Her initial reaction to the explanation that Reese gives is natural enough: uncertainty, doubt, even total disbelief, and this makes her character both convincing and deserving of our sympathies: 'Come on. Do I look like the mother of the future? I mean ... Am I tough? Organised? I can't even balance my chequebook ... Look, Reese, I didn't ask for this honour, and I don't want it ... any of it.'

For a short time she wanders through the film a dazed and confused victim, relying upon Reese to save her from the terminator, upon the police to save her from Reese. But the evidence of her experiences will eventually lead her into acceptance of the facts developed by Reese. However, even when she appears most vulnerable there are signs of a tougher more resilient character. They are developed gradually during the early chase scenes. In order to enable Reese to shoot at the terminator Sarah has to take over the steering of their car. As the vehicles hurtle through the underpass towards the brick wall Sarah slams their car into reverse bringing it to a halt, whilst the terminator's stolen police car hits the wall straight on. She further prevents Reese from suicidally leaping from the car in order to engage the police in more gunfight.

As the film progresses these incidents seem to appear more frequently. The evening they take refuge in the culvert marks something of a transition: she seems to shed the last vestiges of doubt, makes her first field dressing and grows closer to Reese – the shared dream symbolically marking the transformation. She learns willingly how to make pipe bombs, but she is still capable of error, informing the terminator of their position when she mistakenly thinks she is talking to her mother. Comparisons with Ginger also begin to take on a new light. Whilst initially appearing vivacious, Ginger's character later seemed limited; her lovemaking is almost no more

character

Sarah seems genuine in her affection

Sarah and Reese grow closer

than a Walkman accompanied exercise routine. At least Sarah seems genuine in her affection.

There is a clear difference in the Sarah of the later chase scenes: it is she who reminds Reese of the pipebombs as a means of destroying the terminator; and whilst Reese pulled her to safety in the Tech Noir the roles are reversed when she drags him to safety as the terminator rams their upturned pick-up. Towards the end Reese is a fading figure, who has to be barked at by a sudden sergeant-majorish Sarah, 'Move it, Reese. On your feet, soldier'.

Ultimately, she is forced into saving herself. Seemingly cornered in a hopeless position she keeps her nerve and finds the switch that will bring the hydraulic press down on the outreaching figure of her nemesis, spitting out with bold assertion using language that signals her transformation: 'You're ... terminated ... fucker!'

The epilogue reveals the next metamorphosis as a pregnant Sarah, handgun on her lap, drives across the Mexican desert in a jeep marked 'Renegade'. There are signs of a Sarah still perplexed by the whole incident, but there is now total acceptance of what the future will hold as she records tapes of her thoughts for her future son, and prepares with readiness to face the storm that lies ahead.

To Cameron, Sarah's transition is everything:

> For me the important theme dramatically within the film is strictly human and personal. ... It's the idea that the main character is forced into a situation of having to take responsibility for her own fate and her own survival.
>
> *Cameron in Bahiana, 1991, p. 20*

narrative theory & the terminator

Narrative theory is something of a minefield with critics openly divided as to its validity. David Bordwell (1988) has derided the academic exercise as pointless, whilst for others it offers important steps to universal understanding of the significance of narrative.

According to Russian narrative theorist Tzvetan Todorov narrative can be described as happening in three stages. There is usually a state of equilibrium, when all in the social world is as it should be. This is followed by a disruption leading to disequilibrium. In turn the disruption is recognised and there follows an attempt to repair the damage. Finally we see a restoration or return to some kind of equilibrium. Here, according to this pattern, narrative is not defined as a linear structure, but as circular with the restoration of order being a restoration of the equilibrium seen at the beginning, although it does not necessarily have to be the same equilibrium.

There are obvious applications here for *The Terminator*. In common with many narratives there is a disruption, but the sense of equilibrium – represented in Sarah's mundane routine – is held back for reasons of suspense. The disruption – the threat to her life – is recognised and dealt with, and a sense of equilibrium restored, although a very different sense of order has been established at the end, with the added dimension that this cycle will continue in the future with further disruption, albeit one that our character now fully anticipates.

More revealing perhaps are the questions raised by such a model. The notion of equilibrium raises questions about how social order is represented and about how it resists or changes when disruption is applied, and finally how it functions to effect closure within stories.

As Cameron asserts, Sarah's trial is one of having to fight back – hers is a social order that gives her freedom but does not treat her well. She has to take responsibility for her own actions and by doing so she has a say in the future.

We can also see such questions opening up the ideological arguments that underpin the film. The terminator is a machine, albeit as Reese argues – a cyborg, created by machines to destroy humankind. A machine is sent to end all humankind's hope, and yet a machine is used by a human to kill a machine. Just how dependent on machines are we to allow such a concept to be imaginable?

Another narrative approach was outlined in the 1920s by Vladimir Propp in his pathbreaking study *Morphology of the Folktale*. In analysing a number of Russian folktales to see if they shared common properties, Propp discovered that all of them, no matter how different their surface details, shared certain important structural features. Characters, or rather the function of characters became his starting point, and he discovered that they could fit into one of seven types of dramatic personae:

1. The hero, who is the character who seeks something.

2. The villain, who opposes or blocks the hero's quest.

3. The donor, who provides an object which has some magic property.

4. The dispatcher, who sends the hero on his way by providing a message.

5. The helper, who aids the hero.

6. The princess, who acts as reward for the hero and as object of the villain's scheming.

The seventh character function varies according to which interpretation of Propp is followed. Some argue for the existence of the father, who acts to reward the hero for his efforts, others wish to recognise a false hero, who attempts to present themselves as a hero, but whose claims are unfounded. Applying such notions derived from traditional folk tales to contemporary film plots may seem something of a dubious process, and certainly may require some shifting of definitions, but may also yield surprising results.

If we see Reese occupying the hero role, then Sarah clearly serves as the princess, but also gains in importance through her function as helper. The terminator is the obvious villain, but is it stretching the point to see him as a false hero? The donor, the dispatcher and father could all be roles occupied by John Connor, the one character we do not actually see at all during the film. This is a significant development as we may tend to overlook his importance because he does not occupy screen time, and yet in certain respects he is the prime motivator for all that happens: his presence is the motivation for the sending back in time of the terminator, he then subsequently sends back Kyle Reese, in order to protect his mother, and also, with the knowledge we see passed on to him through Sarah, to serve as his own father who, he knows, will die in the process. Thus the narrative suddenly opens up a host of unheralded implications for our understanding of the film's ideology.

Propp further listed thirty-one functions of the plot, broadly categorised as: Preparation, Complication, Transference, Struggle, Return and Recognition. Uncannily many of these elements directly describe events in *The Terminator*, although crucially – often something of a flaw in Propp's proposals – the order varies; but then again, should we expect the sequencing of a plot by a 1980s film director to follow faithfully or coincidentally the plot of Russian fairytales as studied in the 1920s.

What is clear, though, is that for all their science fiction trimmings a universal study of good versus evil is once again being brought before us as yet another David and Goliath struggle. Perhaps also, it should come as no surprise that heroic virtues, such as the ability to stand up for oneself, are yet again being rewarded. Although, of course what is perhaps noticeably different is our modern standpoint that explains just how an audience can further enjoy the antics, however grim, of the villain, or is such a standpoint not necessarily modern at all? After all Propp's analysis provides us with the comfort that the villain will always be punished, so why not enjoy that terror while it exists in the knowledge it will not always exist.

Narrative theories have, in fact, attempted to deal with this ambivalence directly. Claude Levi-Strauss (1966) in examining the nature of primitive myths and legends discovered that regardless of their origin the one thing that they had in common was the function they served for the society:

> Myths were used to deal with the contradictions in experience, to explain the apparently inexplicable, and to justify the inevitable.

reconciling oppositions

> Within myths, contradictions and inequities which could not be resolved in the real world were resolved symbolically. The function of myth was to place those contradictions – between man and his natural environment, for instance, or between life and death – as part of natural existence. Myths negotiated a peace between men and women and their environment so that they could live in it without agonising over its frustrations and cruelties.
>
> *Turner, 1993, p. 72*

According to Levi-Strauss these contradictions are to be found expressed in terms of 'binary oppositions' – sets of mutually exclusive categories. We have already established how *The Terminator*'s use of parallelism brings such oppositions very clearly into focus. If we agree with Levi-Strauss that our lives are full of such opposition, and Cameron, who builds on our acceptance of such tenants, clearly expects us to, it is not too difficult a step to accept such narratives as a means of helping reconcile these oppositions in order to make it easier for us to live with them.

style

Whilst narrative is the driving force for most modern movie goers, there is clearly more to film than just the writing of the screenplay and the pointing of the camera at a group of actors. Although as this Note is written there is a distinct move amongst some directors to strip film making of its trappings in an attempt to create a more basic cinema.

When that story unfolds before us it has been subjected to a whole range of techniques that govern the look and feel of the film, that add atmosphere and tension to the plot, that try to convince us that what should be impossible is perfectly possible, and then, of course, there is the editing process that takes everything done to the film and puts it together in such a way that we are not distracted by any of these things, they are simply an integral part of the overall experience.

Of these techniques the one that we are probably most familiar with is mise-en-scène which in its original French means 'staging an action'. Adapted from its theatrical origins mise-en-scène is used to describe the arrangement of elements within the frame or shot: the setting, lighting, costume and character movement as they are constructed and arranged before the camera. A similar term mise-en-shot may be used to label the way filmed events are filmed, and includes such elements as camera position and movement, the length of the shot and the type and pace of editing.

setting

The Terminator features two main settings, or rather one setting across a division of time: Los Angeles; 1984 and 2029. The futuristic vision of LA belongs to the special visual effects team of Fantasy II and was created at a dynamited steelplant using the left over rubble and imported wrecked cars, fallen telephones and street lights. The effect of these sequences was to be 'impressionistic' and 'stroboscopic' as enormous computerised machines roam the debris strewn remnants of the city, searchlights seeking out pockets of human resistance before laser blasting those who remain. There is very much a monochromatic colouring to these scenes as though all colour has been leeched out of the environment: the rebels dressed in grey camouflage shelter amongst the shadows of grey ruined buildings; the machines, all highly polished chrome-plated metal serve to reflect only the cold blue darkness. Backlit silhouetted shapes form the ruins on the surface, whilst survivors have taken to living underground in dimly lit corridors and cellars. It is a cold colourless environment reflecting a world ruled by machines – lacking in emotion bent only on the task of destruction.

Symbolism creeps further into this setting with its roads paved with human skulls, over which rumble the heavy tank tracks of the machines. This shot is reminiscent of wartime propaganda posters depicting the villainy of the enemy, and it gains credence alongside other reminders of past evils:

```
Reese

        Most of us were rounded up, put in camps ...
        for orderly disposal.

He pushes up the sleeve of his jacket and shows her
a ten digit number etched on the skin of his
forearm. Beneath the numbers is a pattern of lines
like the automatic-pricing marks on product
packages.

Reese (continuing)

        Burned in by laser scan.

(pause)

        Some of us were kept alive ... to work. Loading
        bodies. The disposal ran night and day. We
        were that close to going out forever ...
```

Against this the 1984 version of LA might be expected to be a riot of colour and life, but this is not Cameron's intention. When the terminator and influence of film noir

Reese arrive it is at 1.52 in the early hours of the morning and it is still dark. In fact daylight seems a rare commodity in the film, used most noticeably when we first see Sarah arriving for work; as Sarah and Reese emerge from their night sheltering in the drainage culvert; when the wounded Sarah is stretchered away at the end, and for the epilogue as Sarah drives through the desert.

Its use at the end, when the threat of the terminator is removed, links with Sarah's first appearance on her way to work, and thus acts symbolically to mark the restoration of equilibrium.

Daylight features also in some of the terminator scenes. It is in daylight that the terminator enters the gun shop to take by force the weapons he requires, and the killing of the first Sarah Connor takes place on the porch of her house in broad daylight. The terminator is so driven that it matters not whether it carries out its mission during the day or night.

lighting

Much of the responsibility for how the film looks and for achieving the director's vision on film, falls to the director of photography – in this case Adam Greenberg. Cameron's vision when writing the script was influenced by his fondness for film noir of the forties, an influence Greenberg immediately detected: 'That was exactly how I saw it when I first read the script ... I was aiming for a cool look, lots of dark shadows, strong back light ... a very hard, strong, contrasty look' (Thomas McKelvey Cleaver, 'Adam Greenberg', 1985, p. 50).

In film noir – a style of production usually understood as running from *The Maltese Falcon* in 1941 to *Touch of Evil* in 1958 – a central element of the noir look was the high contrast image, achieved by dispensing with softening fill lighting, preferring instead the harsh, unsoftened key light and the deep shadows it created. Such shadows often served to separate characters from each other and produced unbalanced compositions, by casting oblique shadows or placing grids over faces and furniture. It was an effect designed to unsettle and disorient, often mirroring some dislocation on the part of a film's characters.

There is clear use of such lighting through *The Terminator*, in particular in the terminator's raid on the police station, where it gives itself an advantage by fusing the lights, plunging the place into darkness. External light sources thereby cast shadows of blinds across the characters, Sarah attempts to cloak herself in the shadows beneath a desk, whilst tension rises when a silhouetted figure attempts to break into her hiding place through the glass panelled door.

Ironically, the place we might expect to have a characteristic darkness is the Tech Noir – darkness suggested even in its name, but there are few shadows to hide in here. If anything the nightclub has a fluorescent glare that illuminates everything, giving a certain inevitability to the terminator's finding of Sarah and his subsequent attempt to kill her.

Throughout then we mainly have darkness – LA filmed at night. Financial restrictions – a low budget of $6.4 million – clearly limit a director's choices, and, as a result, dictate how a film will look, but filming at night also creates a specific 'look'. The lighting seems harsh; reflected in the rain soaked streets an uncomfortable fluorescent glare that casts dark shadows. It creates a sense of alienation, a brooding menace and tension, that anything can and will happen, similar to what we find in the New York streets of *Taxi Driver* (1976). It even pervades inside of buildings – Ginger's apartment and kitchen, the motel – so that nowhere seems safe. Of course, darkness is to the terminator's advantage. His point of view shots suggest infra-red, and therefore an ability to penetrate the darkness, which adds a further dimension to its seeming invulnerability. The other main subject for lighting are the actors, and the requirements will vary in order to 'say the right thing about the actor and the character'.

> With Linda, I used very soft, very natural lighting to make the statement about her character. For Michael's character, I used shadows, hard shadows, giving a 'hard edge' to him. For Arnold I was using harsh light that gave a mechanical look, and then a lot of low angles, almost all low angles, to emphasise size.
>
> *Cleaver, 1985, p.51*

lighting style

budgetary constraints

As Greenberg indicates, their presentation of Schwarzenegger's terminator became a vital part of the stylisation process. Cameron originally envisaged the terminator being 'a more anonymous saturnine figure' but Schwarzenegger's casting in the role made such thinking irrelevant. The techniques of film style are used instead to emphasise Schwarzenegger's terminator as different, as huge, as a threat of monsterlike proportions. The lighting emphasises the size of his body and the sharp angles to his face, especially the forehead and cheek bones, creating a skull like effect when caught by the dashboard lights of the stolen police car.

framing

Even the positioning of the camera is used to highlight and exaggerate the terminator's size. One of Greenberg's requirements of shooting was the ability to have the camera on the floor for the extreme low angled shots, since that was the photographic method used to stylise Schwarzenegger as the terminator. 'He's big to begin with, but doing all these low angles makes him look like a monster' (Cleaver, 1985, p. 51).

At one point early on the hand-held camera begins at Schwarzenegger's biker-boot-clad feet and rises slowly to his impassive face, emphasising not only his size but also the aggressiveness of the clothes he has taken from the punks.

Much of the camera work in the film is hand held, reflecting Greenberg's documentary newsreel background: 'to me shooting hand-held gives an energy to a scene you can't get any other way' (Cleaver 1985, p. 51).

Although budgetary constraints precluded the use of Steadicam, Greenberg improvised, creating his own piece of equipment: 'The Adam Camera', which provided Greenberg with the manoeuvrability he required.

Movement throughout the film is highly significant (see Editing), but the tracking shot takes on a particular resonance in several key scenes. When Ginger leaves the sleeping figure of Matt, her boyfriend, to fetch food from the kitchen, she is tracked along the darkened corridor at a particularly low level. The shot precedes her murder at the hands of the terminator, and stylistically resembles slasher films of the horror genre popular from the mid 1970s onwards, the most memorable being John Carpenter's

Halloween. The low angle encapsulates the sexual voyeuristic frisson of being able to look upwards; the tracking movement suggests the threat that could strike at any moment. Likewise in the Tech Noir scene, the camera's ability to track the terminator as it prowls the nightclub heightens the tension.

Even fairly static scenes are invested with a sense of movement. Silberman's questioning of Reese takes place with participants seated around the table. Reese, thinking only of his mission, is very animated, and the camera adds to this by moving around and amongst the seated protagonists.

If the actual handling of the camera is used to emphasise movement and size, the framing of shots is used to trap the characters. Influenced by films like *Das Boot* (1981), which told the story of a U-boat crew on its tour of duty during the Second World War, the framing of *The Terminator* tends to be claustrophobic: close-ups of faces and upper torsos tends to dominate; there are few establishing shots; everything is crammed into the frame. Even the buildings are only partly glimpsed from the outside as characters move in, out or past them. Longer, more distant shots, tend to be restricted to chase scenes, where forward momentum affords little time to take everything in. The effect of this is to intensify what is happening to the characters. There is no release from the frame, just as there appears to be no escape for Reese and Sarah.

The use of close-up also serves to develop the narrative elements within the film. A close-up of the terminator's hand lying still and then moving informs us that the terminator is still very much alive, a similar close-up of the terminator's hand dripping with blood after ripping out the punk's heart serves to represent the very real threat of violence embodied in the character, whilst also mirroring the readiness of the gunslinger in Western films; whilst a close-up of the interlocked fingers belonging to Reese and Sarah signals their union.

There are further representations of violence to be found in the close-up. When the punks first prepare to attack, there is a synchronised flicking of switchblade, each caught in close-up. Indeed the whole scene is a carefully edited study of close-up, giving the violence of the scene a kind of well-executed choreography. Medium close-ups of faces are interspersed with close-ups of knives and gestures. A medium shot shows the terminator punch the punk and raise him from the ground. A big close-up catches the punk's blade as it helplessly falls to the floor. A further two shots sees the terminator lift the punk higher into the air, whilst a separate close-up of the terminator's feet rooted to the ground and the punk's feet hovering above confirm what we imagine we have seen. The punk then falls and we have a close-up of a bloodied arm, at its end a human heart held tightly.

Other acts of violence are covered in a similar way with violence being suggested through camera framing and editing, rather than being shown in its shocking completeness.

The violence of the film is further stylised by the use of slow-motion: a prominent feature of the 1970s films of directors such as Sam Peckinpah – *The Wild Bunch* (1969) and *Cross of Iron* (1977). The almost balletic choreography of violence through the use of slow-motion had become something of a cliché by the mid 1980s. It serves various purposes, but is nevertheless successful in heightening the tension as the terminator closes in on Sarah in the Tech Noir, and the subsequent shoot out is a slowed down, more exciting spectacle allowing us time to take in the separate actions of the three main protagonists. It further serves to heighten the shocking truth of the terminator's mission in the killing of the first Sarah Connor. The drama of the spectacle is further added to by the treatment of sound alongside the slowing down of screen action. Whilst the volume of background sound, such as the disco music, decreases, the sound level of the gun's action is increased. At that moment both slow-motion image and intensified use of selected sounds direct our attention completely to that one particular event.

sound

We can divide sound into two distinct categories: diegetic sound – with its origins located in the story world – includes the voices of the characters and the sounds accompanying objects that we see on screen; non-diegetic sound is external to the world of the story, as in a musical score that has no obvious source in the shot, but is created to accompany the images on screen.

Brad Fiedel, whose approach was to mirror in music the nature of the world of the film, composed the musical score for *The Terminator*. Hence, the score has a relentlessly mechanistic feel that incorporates industrial sounding percussion, haunting violin and discordant use of synthesisers. The very sound of a synthesiser has implications for a science fiction film, as its electronic source helps to define it as a modern instrument and therefore makes it most appropriate for the electronic modern/futuristic world of science fiction. Fiedel's score is more sound than melody, as if to mirror the cold detachment of the unfeeling machine-driven terminator. The machine-like percussion occasionally sounds like a heart beat that has too many beats to be truly human, and it serves to drive the film forward (see Editing), as if to match the unrelenting single minded purpose of the terminator. The mood is broken twice, when Fiedel returns to more conventional melodic scoring of piano and strings for Sarah's first appearance and the later love scene, here tinged with a bittersweet sadness highly appropriate to such a short-lived union founded in extreme circumstances.

The score, however, is not without a theme – a short but instantly recognisable synth motif built over the hypnotic percussive rhythm. If the percussion serves to remind us of the world of the machine, the brief melody of the themed motif signals some kind of hope for mankind.

Such scoring has obvious implications for atmosphere and mood, but it can also work much more directly within the narrative. Early in the film when an unsuspecting Sarah has left her apartment, she arrives in the underground car park to collect her motor scooter. The scene is played for tension, as Sarah looks down the aisles of parked cars as if sensing a presence. No musical score breaks the tension, until the camera pans following Sarah as she leaves the car park on her scooter. The industrial heartbeat motif is heard and the camera continues its pan to reveal a figure inside a parked car. The industrial heartbeat suggests the presence of the terminator, thus raising audience expectations. It is, in fact, Reese whose motives we are still unsure of, and perhaps now we trust even less.

sound style

In creating a diegetic soundtrack the film maker has to select sound that will fulfil a particular function. The sound world of the film is by necessity a clearer, simpler sound world than that of everyday life. Sounds that exist all around us in our everyday situation would be far too distracting were they to occur in the film with the same regularity and volume as real life.

To a film like *The Terminator* this has an immediate advantage, because the cutting out of much extraneous sound leaves us with a stillness that can be haunting, menacing and charged with tension, especially as the terminator himself is largely silent.

Sounds that are made prominent by this process include those associated with weaponry, the car chases and technology, thus helping to enhance the dramatic themes of the film.

Diegetic sound also links with a further aspect of style: editing. Serving as a sound bridge conversations extend beyond their specific scenes, adding a sense of continuity and urgency to the plot. Having murdered Ginger thinking she was Sarah, the terminator overhears Sarah phoning from the Tech Noir. He seeks confirmation that he has killed the wrong person and finds a university pass with a photograph of Sarah. At the moment he examines the pass, a voice declares 'It's her!', and we cut to the police station to find Lieutenant Traxler on the phone to Sarah, at last having made contact with her. He repeats the words he has just said, 'It's her!'.

editing

One of the most significant aspects of *The Terminator* is its use of movement, especially when employed in developing a determined sense of forward momentum. As an action film it has a duty to keep excitement levels high and to keep the audience interested as they move from one high action set piece to another. Furthermore *The Terminator* is a chase film in the tradition of Walter Hill's *The Driver* (1978) and George Miller's *Mad Max II/The Road Warrior* (1981), and as such relies upon the audience sharing in that sensation of driving forward This feeling of momentum runs throughout the film, and is established right at the very outset. It can even be sensed during the film's opening title sequence, where a series of letters, too large to fit fully on screen, overlap from different directions, before appearing in full to form the title only then to disappear backwards into the invisible horizon.

The structuring of the plot is an obvious starting point to create the forward momentum required, but here every aspect of character movement and editing serves that purpose – to give Cameron the wished-for sense of a rollercoaster ride. There is plenty of movement within the plot as we move from one chase to the next, but in the majority of scenes there is some sense of momentum. Scenes regularly begin with a character walking into shot, and end with a character walking out of shot, and if it is not a character then it is a vehicle. On several occasions there is a sense of multiple movements within the shot. Preceding the first Sarah Connor murder is a low level shot of the street outside her house. A toy truck is foregrounded, whilst in the background a young girl pedals along the pavement out of shot; immediately into shot, moving in the opposite direction appears the wheel of a car, crushing the child's truck and announcing the arrival of the terminator.

There are few traditional establishing shots that might slow things down, and the length of shot is varied, but never dwells unnecessarily. The action scenes in particular involve much use of short shot duration and frequent cuts to heighten tension and excitement.

Underpinning all of this is the tightly controlled technique of continuity editing that has the story moving forward in leaps and bounds. One scene ends with Lieutenant Traxler opening his office door in order to face the press. He has not even left through the door when we cut to a shot of a newsreader announcing his statement on the television in front of Sarah as she eats in a pizza restaurant.

At times, even in a film that relies upon speed, editing can be used to create tension by deliberately interfering with the speed of events. Towards the end of the film the terminator commandeers a gasoline tanker and uses it to ram the pick-up, occupied by Sarah and Reese. In real life it would take very little time for the tanker, travelling at speed, to smash into the pick-up but such a dramatic moment with Sarah attempting to drag an unconscious Reese from the vehicle deserves to have the tension wrung out of it to full potential. The multiple piling up of shots taken of the event

from different angles and perspectives makes the moment stretch well
beyond the time it would take in real life.

special effects

It is hardly surprising, given Cameron's interest in film technology, that we
should find some impressive use of special effect in *The Terminator*. As in
many productions, at times the whole making of the film amounts to one
big special effect. In *The Terminator* such effects range from the obvious –
the creation of futuristic LA and its machine weaponry, to the less obvious
– the illusion of speed in the car chases. 'What I did,' Greenberg reveals,
'was have lights on dimmers mounted on cars accompanying us. The lights
would operate faster than the street lights, giving the feeling that we
were going very fast. Actually, the cars were never driven faster than
40 mph, but those lights gave the illusion of an extra 25–30 mph' (Cleaver,
1985, p. 50).

The most recent developments in special effects involve extensive use of
computer-generated imagery, which has become so sophisticated and
visually convincing that virtually any manipulation of image is possible.
Cameron himself has exploited such technology to the full in his filming of
Titanic, and was even there at the outset with his experiments in morphing
trailed in *The Abyss* and made an integral part of the new terminator –
T-1000 – in *Terminator 2: Judgement Day*. In 1984 such technology was
in its infancy and well beyond the limitations of this budget, but directors
like Cameron were always seeking to extend the boundaries of what did
exist and what was affordable.

Much of the futuristic action involved combining live action with
miniatures. The miniatures, such as the Hunter Killer flying vehicles, were
suspended on wires and then operated almost as puppets, the camera
shooting from a stationary position or being moved across and over the
miniature. Rear projection would then be used to combine live action with
the footage of the miniatures.

Sometimes the most up-to-date technology would not always produce the
best effects. Indeed *The Terminator* effects unit opted for the more
outdated Tesla coil apparatus for the production of the lightning bolts that

marked the arrival of the time travellers. The device was originally adapted for use in the 1930s, where it created similar effects for the early *Frankenstein* movies and the original *Flash Gordon* serials.

Undoubtedly the greatest special effects challenge of the film was the terminator itself:

> I was thinking of an indestructible machine, an endo-skeleton design, which had never been filmed as such. We'd had things like *Westworld*, where Yul Brynner's face falls off and there's a transistor radio underneath – which is not visually satisfying, because you don't feel that this mechanism could have been inside making those facial features. So it started from the idea of doing this sort of definitive movie robot, what I've always wanted to see.
>
> *Cameron in French, 1996*

Three fully mechanised life-sized representations of Schwarzenegger's head were used for the scene which featured the removal of the terminator's eye and for his later disintegration after being run over. A lifelike prosthetic arm was created incorporating working mechanical parts. It was worn like a glove by an extra – a young female flautist – who possessed appropriate dexterity to handle it. The whole scene featuring the terminator operating upon itself by repairing its arm and removing its eye, was skilfully shot using the false body parts and real actors. The finished product was convincing enough to provoke feelings of shock and disbelief; careful cutting suggesting more than was actually shown.

The final version of the terminator we see in the film returns us to Cameron's original vision of a skeletal robot emerging from flames. The finished version was faithful to Cameron's idea and featured only a few modifications by makeup effects expert Stan Winston. Several scale models of the endo-skeleton were produced, including a life-sized puppet that corresponded to Schwarzenegger's proportions. Stop-motion photography was used to bring the skeleton to life, with the life-sized models used for close-ups. A neat touch of continuity is that the endo-skeleton walks with the same limp acquired by the Schwarzenegger terminator when it was run over by the gasoline tanker.

contexts

industrial

In order to fully understand the success of a film like *The Terminator* it is necessary to place the film in a business context. Having referred to the film as low budget, that $6.4 million has to have come from somewhere, and there has to be an industry behind the film-making process that is prepared to invest such sums in the hope of making a return.

The American film industry has never remained in a particularly stable state for any length of time. Like any business-run commodity it is subject to competition; it has to react to whatever economic conditions are prevalent; it has to struggle and manoeuvre to establish and retain control from various parties, both outside and within, and it has to play the cat and mouse game of earning government support and resisting government interference.

In its Hollywood heyday from the 1920s to the 1940s the American film industry was structured in what is known as the studio system. The Big Five studios were: 20th Century Fox, MGM, Paramount, Warner Brothers and RKO. Their control virtually amounted to a monopoly: they ran production, distribution and, through their ownership of movie theatres, exhibition. Also in existence were the Little Three: Columbia, Universal and United Artists. They were made 'little' because they lacked the all important ownership of theatres, where the real profits could be made.

From 1945 onwards this system met a number of challenges that would produce decades of radical change. The challenges ranged from declining audiences through to artistic director-orientated projects versus the iron grip of the money men and studio bosses. European cinema, with its auteur theory, provided an alternative model to further challenge the conservative studio system with its emphasis upon stars and happy endings. The final blows came courtesy of the government and the Justice

Department, which ran a series of legal suits charging the studios with conspiracy to restrain and monopolise trade through a variety of restrictive practices in the distribution and exhibition of films.

When the studios agreed to sell off their theatres chains and end various restricted practices they were forced into a position of abandoning both contracted staff and permanent studio facilities. This in turn led to the setting up of independent production companies, run by the more powerful people, who having lost their own contracts, who would employ, on short-term contracts, others less powerful who had also lost their contracts. The main advantage that independent producers had was the ability to make films more cheaply than the major studios. The main problem that independent producers had was getting finance and distribution to the movie theatres. As independent companies were often set up for only short periods – one or two projects – banks were not exactly forthcoming. Thus was born the relationship between the independents and major studios that still exist today. The majors retain the power to obtain appropriate finance and their long-standing distribution trains enable them to deliver the product, the independently produced film, to the public.

One of the disadvantages of this new system was the loss of the studio B units, which had been the place to test and train the big names of the future. Directors of the future no longer had a career structure to aspire to. It was with hard work and perseverance that the directors of the future made their way from amateur projects through to underground films and exploitation movies, typified by the works of Roger Corman. They may have gained some artistic freedom along the way, but they still had to please the majors responsible for the ultimate funding and delivery of the project.

The main studios continued to fund their own projects, often concentrating on the blockbusters, convinced by the notion that only the most expensive films could make big profits. The down side to this being quite naturally, the bigger the cost, the bigger the loss. Production costs rose from an average of $2 million in 1972 to $10 million in 1980 and $23 million in 1989. On average a further $10 million were needed for advertising and prints.

industrial

With such high fees involved the majors sought some guarantees of success and found this in the big stars, who most visibly replaced the old studio identity and subsequent audience loyalty. The stars came with their own price tags, now being in a far more advantageous position to negotiate their fees per movie, rather than being contracted long term to a studio.

Sequels, too, provided some guarantee of profitability by capitalising on the initial success of an original idea, thus it is hardly surprising to find a preponderance of sequels from the 1970s onwards.

The market being much more competitive and hazardous ensured more takeovers and mergers, with companies further looking to diversify into publishing and music. The success of television with its insatiable demands provided other opportunities just as it changed the cinema audience forever. Where once there had been the accepted notion of the movie going family audience, there was a fragmented, suburban, youthful audience whose wide-ranging tastes would not always be satisfied by traditional fare.

Other advances in technology were to follow, most noticeably the growth of home video. In 1980 only around two of every hundred American homes owned a video cassette recorder; ten years later, about two-thirds did. Today, home video can account for up to one-third of the total revenue of a major studio.

The independents had never had it so good, potential markets being the cinema itself, television and the home video audience. Companies entered the business knowing that even a modest picture could recoup most of its costs from the pre-sale of distribution rights to pay cable and home video.

It was within this system of independent companies working with major studios for production costs and distribution that *The Terminator* came to be born.

production history

Having dreamt the initial idea and written the original screenplay Cameron had then to sell his idea. At the time he was writing and living with Gale

THE TERMINATOR

production history

Anne Hurd, whom Cameron had met and briefly worked with at Corman's New World. Hurd's speciality was production and, having bought *The Terminator* screenplay from Cameron for a dollar, she set about trying to sell it to the studios – their contract stipulating that Cameron should direct.

Even a relatively successful independent film system could not guarantee take-up of every idea that came its way, and so with *The Terminator*. It suffered rejection after rejection until it finally met someone who showed interest in the project.

John Daly, a Cockney dock worker, had formed a partnership with the actor David Hemmings, creating in the process a talent agency called Hemdale. The company became successful and diversified into music, TV and movie representation. Daly bought Hemmings's share and moved the business to Hollywood as yet another independent production company. Cameron, aware that his opportunities were limited knew that he had to capitalise on Daly's initial interest quickly and effectively. He enlisted the help of his friend the actor, Lance Henrikson, who was later to play the cop Vukovich:

> I went in to Hemdale and Jim had planned it so I would get there about half an hour ahead of him. I went in decked out like the terminator. I put gold foil from the Vantage cigarette package in my teeth and waxed my hair back. Jim had put fake cuts on my head. I wore a ripped-up punk rock T-shirt, a leather jacket, and boots up to my knee. It was a really exciting look. I was a scary person to be in a room with. I kicked the door open when I got there and the poor secretary just about swallowed her typewriter. I headed in to see the producer. I sat in the room with him and I wouldn't talk with him. I just kept looking at him. After a few minutes of that he was ready to jump out of the window.
>
> *Lance Henrikson in Heard, 1997, p. 63*

Cameron's pitch saw him impress Daly further with detailed sketches of various sequences of the screen play. Daly agreed to back the movie with the resources of Hemdale Films. He subsequently made a distribution deal with Orion Pictures.

Orion's indifference

Orion, as if deliberately wielding the power of the distributor, adapted their own marketing strategy almost in ignorance of what Cameron was about: they compressed all the advertising budget into the final week before the release, holding only one preview and promoting the film as if it were a *Dirty Harry* (1971) knock-off with a science fiction twist.

When the movie was finished Cameron was shocked by Orion's indifference:

> This guy from Orion was downright dismissive of the movie. He told me that a down-and-dirty little action thriller like this usually lasts about three weeks. Box office drops by 50 per cent by the second week and then it completely vanishes by the third ... Even after the initial success, which was even more than I expected, they still had no interest in beefing up the ad campaign or giving it any added support at all. They treated me like dogshit.
>
> *Cameron in Heard, 1997, pp. 76–7*

The initial success was largely based upon some positive press reviews and much word of mouth, but for Cameron the positive feelings of success were short lived when a lawsuit suddenly appeared suggesting that the film borrowed heavily on two scripts for *Outer Limits* and a short story *I Have No Mouth and I Must Scream*, all written by the prodigious science fiction author Harlan Ellison. Ellison's reaction opens up many questions of a post-modern society that draws upon anything and everything for its influences, especially long-standing science fiction concepts of time travel, nuclear holocausts and world dominating machines without actually depending upon any one particular source. Cameron was adamant about the universal nature of his ideas, but Hemdale and Orion, eager to avoid a public and costly fight, would only back him so far – if he won. If Ellison won they promised to sue Cameron. Cameron reluctantly gave in and prints of the film were reissued crediting the works of Harlan Ellison, whilst the author himself was rewarded with approximately $400,000 in compensation.

Despite this setback the film established Cameron as a script writer and director to watch. A reputation he was to build on in his subsequent films,

ideology

elevating him to probably the most powerful director of action movies to date. His direction of *The Terminator* would be highly praised by critics and audience alike, appreciative of what he had been able to achieve on a relatively low budget.

In many respects it was the action adventure film that had everything, and therefore had a universal appeal. Furthermore without the hype and with minimum advance publicity it allowed the audience to feel that they were discovering something for themselves.

ideology

No artist works in a vacuum. Films are always products of their time, even if cloaked in distant historical garb or flush with the trappings of an imagined future. Either consciously or unconsciously they build upon and deal with ideas about their time. This relationship may occasionally take the form of a straightforward statement, but in the main it is complex and problematic. Even in films whose ideological intentions are made clear through statements made by its participants, the finished product may offer a variety of possible readings, some of which may be seen to directly contradict those original intentions.

> The most highly successful and broadly popular movies of this era are best understood as ideological fantasies about the relationship of the American nation to the realities and implications of its own recent history
>
> *Nowell-Smith, 1996, p. 516*

In certain respects North America's recent history since the Second World War has been one of great stability. Emerging as one of the world's superpowers it has held fast to its position, whilst other nations have inwardly folded and collapsed. Its cultural and ideological takeover of the world has been almost low key, but has given it a dominance that others can only envy.

This is, however, only part of the picture. America's recent history has also been witness to political assassinations and to political scandal and

ideology

corruption typified by Watergate in the early 1970s. America's foreign policy was dogged by often spectacular disaster, in particular the traumatic experience of defeat in Vietnam.

Islamic anti-American feeling throughout the Middle East and Asia had further fuelled resistance to dominant American imperialism. On the home front too America had to face upheaval and change, brought about by the newly militant demands of women and 'minority groups' (racial, ethnic and sexual), who sought equality and a greater say in all aspects of society.

For Joseph Sartelle the big blockbuster films of the late 1970s and early 1980s responded to the social and political developments by denying them. *Star Wars* distanced itself in time and location – 'a long time ago, in a galaxy far, far away'; the Indiana Jones movies offered the moral certainties of 1930s Nazi villainy; *Back to the Future* took refuge in the nostalgia of the 1950s American suburbs and *Close Encounters of the Third Kind* look to the skies and extra-terrestrial intervention. However, Sartelle also notices an ambivalence in these films that links them with the action adventure films of the same period: 'What they had in common was a commitment to reviving American self-confidence through reimagining the strong white male hero' (Nowell-Smith, 1996, p. 518).

This mood of aggressive reimagining was further mirrored in the political arena, in which a Hollywood B-movie star had made the Presidency his own: '[Ronald] Reagan's world was like an old Hollywood movie; he saw things in simple terms of right and wrong, with the Communists as the bad guys and the West leading a "crusade of freedom"' (Isaacs and Downing, 1998, p. 333).

Both Hollywood and Reagan sought to lift the American people out of their problematic past by persuading them to have faith in their own abilities. The focus was clearly upon the individual and the individual's ability to change things by taking some definite action in the fight for what was right, the most obvious cinematic representation of Reagan's aggression being the early action adventure films featuring Sylvester Stallone's *Rambo*. Born of the rogue cop films of Clint Eastwood and Charles Bronson, *Rambo* epitomised the power of the individual solving political and personal problems through a combination of musculature and extensive firearms. Its epitome is perhaps the biggest-grossing film of the mid 1980s, the highly jingoistic *Top Gun* (1986).

By the mid 1980s even the Reagan era had fallen victim to scandal, its aggressive foreign policy ultimately being its undoing with the Iran-Contra scandal. The world Reagan had stood for and against was itself beginning to change. The Cold War that had dominated relations between the superpowers was coming to an end. At home the political neglect of domestic problems demanded a greater focus on internal social responsibilities. Hollywood also found itself changing: 'big action films were replaced by a more grim, violent and survivalist sensibility – as though the American experience in Vietnam was now being replayed in internal and domestic terms' (Nowell-Smith, 1996, p. 518).

Indeed, for some *The Terminator* itself is a direct metaphysical commentary upon the contemporary political situation:

> On grounds deeper than mere empathy, we see in Kyle a viable representation of the political body of the American 1980s. He is scarred in soul and body by a foreign war (if we read the future, like the past, as another country); it is also a war it is clear 'we' should by moral rights win (or have been allowed to have won); and it's a war whose continuing legacy is evident in attempts literally to rewrite the past (making 'T1' a subtle compliment to the gross revisionism of the Rambo films). And it is a body, literally neglecting its domestic health for expenditures on defense.
>
> *Larson, 1997, p. 61*

Written in the early 1980s, filmed and released in the mid 1980s *The Terminator* seems to straddle both the Reagan and post-Reagan influence. Cameron clearly shares in the view that the individual has the power to shape and change things, but the emergence of Sarah Connor as the individual in question would suggest a sensibility more in tune with the social upheavals of the 1960s and 1970s. This view is further complicated by the fact that the muscles and firepower of the film belong more to the villain than to the heroes. Neither is this a patriotic view. Cameron seems to question all forms of authority: the government conspires with big business to hand over the fate of humankind to machines; the police force seem singularly ineffective at their task; intellectuals, such as the criminal psychologist Silberman seem interested only in their own self-promotion. It is one of the film's grimmest ironies that Silberman, the one character we truly come to dislike, escapes the annihilation of the police station. At times *The Terminator* holds obvious criticisms of Reaganite politics. In the film the cause of the nuclear war, that places humankind on the verge of destruction, is the computer defence system – SKYNET, an obvious reference to Reagan's own Strategic Defense Initiative – Star Wars. Reagan's vision was of a defensive shield that would intercept and destroy incoming hostile missiles by use of laser beams in space. The very idea of such a shield threatened to undo the nuclear balance at a time when relationships between East and West were thawing, and had it ever come into being would have most probably escalated the nuclear arms build up beyond any hope of compromise.

Not all of the film's ideological stance, however, is so clear cut. What is clear is that the film allows a series of ambiguous, often conflicting, interpretations that, like the story itself, seem several alternating points of view:

> It can be argued that *The Terminator* is another Reagan-era anti-abortion film in which a single woman wisely decides to have her baby rather than terminate her pregnancy. ... But I believe Cameron and Hurd think of Sarah as an independent, leftist woman of the sixties and seventies, an era when unmarried women, who gave birth to and raised their children, stood in defiance of the pro-nuclear family political right. ... Sarah giving birth to John Connor is a political as well as a personal act; she has decided to give birth to a future revolution that is necessitated by anti-humanity policies undertaken in her own time, our time – the Reagan years.

> *Peary, 1998, p. 236*

As evidence for his view Danny Peary leans heavily upon Lillian Necakov's article 'The Terminator; Beyond Classical Hollywood Narrative'. Both Peary and Necakov find convincing supporting evidence in the film's narrative and style. *The Terminator*, with its paramilitary outfit, aggressive attitude and predilection for weaponry is 'the embodiment of macho and a male dominated world, and in a sense an extreme right-wing world' (Necakov, 1987, p. 86). Reese is a new breed of hero, clearly human, clearly vulnerable and yet capable of the heroic. In the shot of Reese sawing off the end of his shotgun Necakov finds clear symbolism, 'this seems important in view of the whole macho image of men. Reese is not afraid to "shorten his phallus", as it were, whereas the Terminator needs as many guns as he can get' (Necakov, 1987, p. 86). It is ultimately his relationship with Sarah, and Sarah's transformation throughout the film, that forms the crux of Necakov's argument. As a guerrilla fighter in the future Reese works alongside women who match his courage and bravery. It is these qualities in Sarah, as related to him by John Connor, that have attracted Reese and lead to his voluntary returning back in time 'to meet the legend'. He offers protection, but expects Sarah to be an equal – to drive, to handle a gun and to make bombs.

As for Sarah, her transformation is one of the main narrative structures of the film. It is to these liberating elements that Necakov is drawn – signs of strength and independence that show Sarah transcending 'gender role expectations'. She is a character with a sense of humour – patting the 'male' statue in front of the burger restaurant, 'Guard it for me, big buns'. When stood up by her date she is prepared to go out on her own, and she is quite prepared to demand that the television news is left on when a bar full of men decide to change channels. She drives herself around, her ownership and use of the moped paralleling her with the only other motorcyclist in the film – the terminator itself. When Sarah and Reese make love, it is Sarah who initiates it, and it is Sarah who takes the 'dominant' position. During such scenes it is often the woman who is sexually objectified, and yet while both characters are clearly naked, it is Reese who spends most of the scene half-undressed. Of course at the film's climax it is Sarah who destroys the terminator – a fact that for Necakov makes 'the transference the power to Sarah even more subversive'. Furthermore, at the very end of the film Sarah is alone and pregnant, prepared to face the future without a partner:

the need for love

'The gun she carries at the film's end symbolises the power she has obtained'.

Margaret Goscilo in 'Deconstructing The Terminator' (1987–8), however, argues against these liberating progressive interpretations of the film. She takes issue with Necakov arguing that whilst the film 'accommodates' shifts in gender inflections it is far less radical than Necakov suggests, and what Necakov finds as unwelcomingly subversive is actually undermined by narrative and genre conventions. By deliberately holding back the reasons for the hunting down and killing of Sarah Connor, the narrative clearly places Sarah in the thankless role of damsel in distress. The whole build-up of characterisation through this narrative suspense serves further to subordinate Sarah. Goscilo argues that the portrayal of Sarah at work clearly signals her incompetence, even helplessness, whilst the male characters, in particular the terminator, are dynamic and purposeful 'the very embodiment of ruthless male potency on a mysterious mission'. Goscilo's comparing of Reese to Sarah deepens this gulf. The character of Reese is gradually fleshed out by the use of future-flashback and this, Goscilo argues, is 'enough to subordinate Sarah, who is never afforded such inner portrayal – enough, in fact, to make Reese far more the subject of the narrative than Sarah, who, despite her nominal importance, functions as its object' (Goscilo, 1987–8, p. 40). For Goscilo the early suggestions of Sarah's independence are subtly undercut by a need for love. Her present date stands her up, leaving a gap – an 'eloquent' signalling of Reese's possible role in the near future. Sarah, herself, invites such a reading as, after hearing her date's message on the answering machine, she hugs her per lizard and jokes, 'Pugsley still loves me'. Her interactions with Pugsley are further interpreted by Goscilo as signs of Sarah's maternal instincts, marking a destiny that 'verges on the stereotype of woman as breeder'. Her initiating of their lovemaking is furthermore, Goscilo argues, more of a reaction to the man's interest than the operation of a woman's desire.

And whilst, for Necakov, Sarah's possession of the gun in the final scene denoted the power she had gained, for Goscilo, its obvious phallicism serves to symbolise the overarching domination of the male throughout the film, subsuming in the process Sarah's heroism.

ideology

The presence of guns throughout opens up more questions of the film's ideological stance, similarly along the lines of the film's ambiguities. In the gunshop scene the ease with which the terminator arms itself with sophisticated weaponry verges on the satirical. The irony of having to wait fifteen days for a handgun, whilst the machine guns can be carried away immediately, would appear to give great credence to a pro-gun control stance. Yet at the end of the film a gun symbolically rests on Sarah's pregnant bell as if to confound such a notion.

For Sean French (1996) the film's distrust of authority also brings a darker meaning to the ideology of the film. Whilst in Britain such distrust is usually seen as being typical of left-wing beliefs, in the United States it is also fundamental to right-wing militancy, with its deep distrust of virtually all forms of social organisation and control, and its firm belief in the power of the gun. As French reminds us, we need look no further than the Oklahoma City bombing to see the potential threat of such ideologies.

The violence of the film has also inevitably attracted much media attention in the long-standing debate about the potential influence of cinema violence of the viewer. For Cameron:

> If you're doing an action film, there's no real difference between action and violence: action is violence, violence is action. It is just a question of the tone and style of how it's handled ... I believe you can't have an action film without what is essentially a violent situation. So then the question is; what kind of violence? Are we talking about graphic violence, blood spattering in slow-motion, that sort of thing?
>
> *Cameron in Bahiana, 1991, p. 85*

In *The Terminator* there is a sense of Cameron exploring his medium and that includes the portrayal of violence. At times it appears choreographed through careful editing, it indulges for dramatic purposes in the cliché of slow-motion and the comic book excesses of scenes such as the terminator taking on the police department. It is a highly stylised portrayal, that more often than not looks away at the crucial moment, preferring not to glorify violence, but to accept its inevitable significance in the plot.

In some respects *The Terminator* is as much about aggression as it is violence, and as much of this is from human characters as it is from the terminator itself. Cameron leaves us in no doubt that we do not always compare favourably to a remorseless uncaring machine. It is the three punks who attempt to intimidate the terminator. Sarah gains little sympathy, but a large portion of hostility as she muddles her way through her job, and a biker at a phone booth demands of his 'baby', 'I don't care what you are doing, come and get me!' before taking issue with the terminator, 'Hey man. You've got a serious attitude problem'.

As if in direct contrast to such attitudes are those interpretations that seek to highlight the potential religious allusions of the film in particular as an allegory relating to the Nativity. Sarah represents the Virgin Mary. Reese act as the annunciatory angel, who goes one step further impregnating Sarah herself. The terminator can be seen both as Herod, slaughtering this time not the first born but the Sarah Connors, and as a Satan figure, for Sean French famously recalling Milton's characterisation in *Paradise Lost*, 'who by attempting to destroy humanity perversely brings about its salvation'. (French, 1996, p. 50). The allusion is completed by the figure of John Connor, a Jesus Christ figure charged with the task of saving humanity. Is it mere incident that John Connor and Jesus Christ should share the same initials, or it is more significant that an often playful James Cameron should join them in this too?

intertextuality

The theme of time travel is a long-standing science fiction theme and forms a central element to a narrative of *The Terminator*. H.G. Wells is usually credited as being the first to 'pierce eternity' with *The Time Machine* in 1895. The idea of moving in time was not a new one, but was usually a matter of moving soul or mind, rather than physically moving the body of the traveller. Wells proposed the creation of a machine to enable the traveller to undertake the journey, and thus gave birth to what has become a common concept in our literature of the imagination.

The Terminator uses the concept as a plot device, enabling the future to meet with the past in an attempt to influence that self-same future. Such notions are not without complications and *The Terminator* is no exception. What is significant is that Cameron does not completely dodge the issues: he has his characters convincingly bewildered; a frustrated Reese 'I don't know the tech stuff' and a struggling Sarah, 'You know, you could go crazy thinking about this'.

Cameron's understanding of pace insists that the audience, instead of questioning the more problematic paradoxes, share in and accept such points of view, thus overcoming any potential obstacles to enjoyment.

Of much greater significance is the dystopian view of a world dominated by machines. Again, an idea we may consider to be most modern actually is rooted in science fiction's much deeper past. As far back as Jules Verne the dangers of a machine reliant culture were quite evident: 'if men go on inventing machinery they'll end up by being swallowed up by their own machines' (*Five Weeks in a Balloon*, 1863). Anticipating *The Terminator's* own central promise Samuel Butler in *Erewhon* (1872) had argued that, by a process of mechanical evolution, machines might develop consciousness, enslave man and finally supersede him. Indeed, the very inventor of the term robot, the Czech writer Karl Capek foresaw in his *R.U.R* (1921) a world in which robot slaves would rise up and eradicate their masters.

The film's central figure is the embodiment of all such fears, but our society's reliance upon machines and the fallibility of technology is a message that informs the film at every level: when needed most telephones are out of order; when necessity is at its most demanding phone lines are jammed; telephones are further used to deceive, bleepers distract at a vital moment, and answer machines serve only to give away information that could ultimately lead to death.

Of course such ideas reach well beyond their science fiction roots finding an all-too immediate importance in present reality.

In his article 'Termination or Transformation?', Robert F. Arnold (1998)

a machine saves the day

examines the political and sociological significance of the automated factory. Here, he finds *The Terminator* acting as a metaphor for society's relationship with its high-tech industrial assembly lines, which threaten 'to terminate workers' jobs and rights, and which the robot terminator symbolically represents' (p. 25.)

Ideological ambiguity is again a feature of the film as the terminator is destroyed in a moment of wonderful irony, by another machine, the hydraulic press. Thus having spent much time pointing out the dangers of our overdependence upon machines that let us down and betray us, the film relies upon our use of them in defeating the protagonist. After all of its criticism the ending justifies our dependence on machines in grave situations.

filmography

Cameron's ideas are nothing new, as he himself is quick to acknowledge. He draws upon a long tradition of films that deal with the theme of man and machine.

One of the very classic science fiction movies features a strikingly familiar motif. In Fritz Lang's *Metropolis* (1925) we see an early antecedent of the cyborg terminator, in the form of the feminoid robot creation, the evil double of the saintly Maria. In a scene that very much prefigures Cameron's nightmare vision we see the burning away of surface flesh to reveal the robot beneath.

In *The Day the Earth Stood Still* (1951) we find one of science fiction cinema's most impressive robotic creations in the form of Gort – an imposing giant figure capable of vaporising men and machinery at the slightest hint of provocation. Religious illusions abound: Klaatu the human-like space traveller, attempts to gain a human viewpoint by taking the name of Carpenter and taking up residence in a guest house. He is killed and then returns to life with messages of how humankind may find salvation. Rather ominously, Klaatu proposes the use of robots, such as Gort, to maintain law and order.

James Cameron cites *Westworld* (1974) as a direct influence. The robots of a futuristic entertainment complex are meant to interact with the human

filmography

clients, but a virus causes them to malfunction causing them to slaughter the paying customers. Again, in the world of science fiction, technology turns upon its human creators, but, for Cameron, there was a technology here that he wished to build upon and better. When unmasked the robot beneath seems unconvincing. For Cameron the creation of a convincing robot, both on the surface and beneath, became a primary aim of his own robot film.

Further science fiction films made use of robots: some intended to be cute as in *Silent Running* (1972); some characters in their own right as in R2–D2 and C3PO of *Star Wars* fame; some even foreshadowing the eventual threat of the terminator – *Saturn 3* (1980) proffering a robot with its own sexual desire and a determination to fulfil its needs.

George Lucas's *THX 1138* (1970) depicted a grim dystopian view of an emotionless underground world, where individuality and sexual intercourse are crimes enforced by police uniform-attired robots.

Perhaps, *Alien* (1979) came closest to pre-empting Cameron in his aim. The character Ash, is revealed as a robot working for the self-serving interest of the Company and against the dreadful plight of his human companions. Towards the end of the film he is destroyed and appears in broken form, but Ash is more organic than mechanical, and Cameron was aiming for a definite skeletal look, 'I'd never really seen a good robot in a movie, ever. Not a really great one the way they used to be portrayed on the covers of "Analog" where robots had a waist like an insect so you knew it could not be a guy in a suit' (Cameron in Brosnan, 1991, p. 241).

The replicants of *Blade Runner* (1982) are not robots but genetically engineered human constructs, who serve as slaves and disposable soldiers to a universe colonising humankind. As with many consciousness-developing robots the replicants have virtually no choice other than to question the role they serve and their built-in obsolescence, ultimately having no choice but to act against those who would seek to control them.

Computers also served to threaten their human creators. Most famously the malfunctioning HAL in *2001: A Space Odyssey* (1968) and the less well-known Colossus of *The Forbin Project* (1969) – a giant computer designed to take control of the US defence network, but with personal ambitions of its own.

The robot film of course did not finish with *The Terminator*. Film makers have continued to explore the relationship between humankind and its machines, some like *Robocop* (1987) and *Hardware* (1990) might well be indebted to Cameron who returned to rework his own idea in the inevitable sequel *Terminator 2: Judgement Day* (1991). None, however, apart from Cameron's own work have managed to repeat the success of *The Terminator* either financially or critically. None possess that all-important combination of vision and talent that seem to infect all levels of the film from crew through to cast, elevating in the process the reputation of its director and star, and producing a film that is still mentioned with excitement by new audiences today.

bibliography

general film

Altman, Rick, *Film Genre*,
BFI, 1999
  Detailed exploration of film genres

Bordwell, David, *Narration in the Fiction Film*, Routledge, 1985
  A detailed study of narrative theory and structures

– – –, Staiger, Janet & Thompson, Kristin, *The Classical Hollywood Cinema: Film Style & Mode of Production to 1960*, Routledge, 1985; pbk 1995
  An authoritative study of cinema as institution, it covers film style and production

– – – & Thompson, Kristin, *Film Art*, McGraw-Hill, 4th edn, 1993
  An introduction to film aesthetics for the non-specialist

Branson, Gill & Stafford, Roy, *The Media Studies Handbook*, Routledge, 1996

Buckland, Warren, *Teach Yourself Film Studies*, Hodder & Stoughton, 1998
  Very accessible, it gives an overview of key areas in film studies

Cook, Pam (ed.), *The Cinema Book*, BFI, 1994

Corrigan, Tim, *A Short Guide To Writing About Film*, HarperCollins, 1994
  What it says: a practical guide for students

Dyer, Richard, *Stars*, BFI, 1979; pbk Indiana University Press, 1998
  A good introduction to the star system

Easthope, Antony, *Classical Film Theory*, Longman, 1993
  A clear overview of recent writing about film theory

Hayward, Susan, *Key Concepts in Cinema Studies*, Routledge, 1996

Hill, John & Gibson, Pamela Church (eds), *The Oxford Guide to Film Studies*, Oxford University Press, 1998
  Wide-ranging standard guide

Lapsley, Robert & Westlake, Michael, *Film Theory: An Introduction*, Manchester University Press, 1994

Maltby, Richard & Craven, Ian, *Hollywood Cinema*, Blackwell, 1995
  A comprehensive work on the Hollywood industry and its products

Mulvey, Laura, 'Visual Pleasure and Narrative Cinema' (1974), in *Visual and Other Pleasures*, Indiana University Press, Bloomington, 1989
  The classic analysis of 'the look' and 'the male gaze' in Hollywood cinema. Also available in numerous other edited collections

Nelmes, Jill (ed.), *Introduction to Film Studies*, Routledge, 1996
  Deals with several national cinemas and key concepts in film study

Nowell-Smith, Geoffrey (ed.), *The Oxford History of World Cinema*, Oxford University Press, 1996
  Hugely detailed and wide-ranging with many features on 'stars'

Thomson, David, *A Biographical Dictionary of the Cinema*,
Secker & Warburg, 1975
   Unashamedly driven by personal taste, but often stimulating

Truffaut, François, *Hitchcock*,
Simon & Schuster, 1966,
rev. edn, Touchstone, 1985
   Landmark extended interview

Turner, Graeme, *Film as Social Practice*, 2nd edn, Routledge, 1993
   Chapter four, 'Film Narrative', discusses structuralist theories of narrative

Wollen, Peter, *Signs and Meaning in the Cinema*,
Viking, 1972
   An important study in semiology

Readers should also explore the many relevant websites and journals. *Film Education* and *Sight and Sound* are standard reading.

Valuable websites include:

The Internet Movie Database at
http://uk.imdb.com

Screensite at
http://www.tcf.ua.edu/screensite/contents.html

The Media and Communications Site at the University of Aberystwyth at
http://www.aber.ac.uk/~dgc/welcome.html

There are obviously many other university and studio websites which are worth exploring in relation to film studies.

the terminator

Arnold, Robert, F., 'Termination or Transformation?', *Film Quarterly*, Autumn 1998

Bahiana, Ana Maria, 'Terminator 2', *Cinema Papers*, no. 84, August 1991

Benidt, Jennifer, 'The Terminator', *Cinefex*, 21 April 1985

Bernardin, Marc, 'Terminator', *Creative Screenwriting*, Winter 1995

Brosnan, John, *The Primal Screen*, Orbit, London, 1991

Chute, David, 'Three Guys in Three Directions', *The 1984 Movie Review*, 1985

Cleaver, Thomas McKelvey, 'Adam Greenberg on The Terminator', *American Cinematographer*, April 1985

Clute, John, and Nicholls, Peter, *The Encyclopedia of Science Fiction*, St Martin's Press, New York, 1993

Corman, Roger, with Jerome, Jim, *How I Made a Hundred Movies in Hollywood and Never Lost a Dime*, Random Century Group, London, 1990

French, Sean, *The Terminator*, BFI Modern Classics, British Film Institute, London, 1996

Goscilo, Margaret, 'Deconstructing The Terminator', *Film Criticism*, Winter 1987–8

Heard, Christopher, *Dreaming Aloud: The Life and Films of James Cameron*, Doubleday, Ontario, 1997

Hill, Douglas, *Major Themes taken from Encyclopedia of Science Fiction*, Robert Holdstock (ed.), Octopus, London, 1978

Hillier, Jim, *The New Hollywood*, Studio Vista, London, 1993

Hoberman, J., 'Nietzsche's Boy', *Sight and Sound*, 1991

Isaacs, Jeremy, and Downing, Taylor, *Cold War*, Bantan Press, London, 1998

Jones, Alan, 'James Cameron's Judgement Day', *Starburst*, no. 159, November 1991

Konigsberg, Ira, *The Complete Film Dictionary*, Bloomsbury, London, 1998

Larson, Doran, 'Machine as Messiah: Cyborgs, Morphs, and The American Body Politic', *Cinema Journal*, Summer 1997

Lusted, David (ed.), *The Media Studies Book*, Routledge, London, 1991

McKee, Robert, *Story, Substance, Structure, Style and the Principles of Screenwriting*, Methuen, London, 1998

Naughton, John, *The Terminator in The 10 Definitive Science Fiction Films of All Time*, An Empire Magazine Supplement, 1997

– – –, 'The 12 Best Movies Ever Made?', *Empire*, November 1993

Neale, Steve, and Smith, Murray (eds), *Contemporary Hollywood Cinema*, Routledge, London, 1998

Necakov, Lillian, 'The Terminator: Beyond Classical Hollywood Narrative', *CineAction!*, Spring 1987

Parisi, Paula 'Tools and Jim', *Hollywood Reporter*, March 1995

Peary, Danny, *Cult Movies Three*, Sidgwick and Jackson, London, 1988

Penley, Constance, 'Time Travel, Primal Scene and The Critical Dystopia', *Camera Obscura*, Fall 1986

Perlman, Martin, 'The Terminator', *Cinefantastique*, July 1985

Price, Stuart, *Media Studies*, Pitman Publishing, London, 1994

– – –, *Communication Studies*, Longman, Essex, 1996

Pyle, Forest, 'Making Cyborgs, Making Humans: of Terminators and Blade Runners', *Film Theory Goes to Movies*, Routledge, London, 1993

Richardson, John H., 'Iron Jim', *Premiere*, August 1994

Stein, Michael Eric, 'The New Violence on Twenty Years of Violence in Films: An Appreciation', *Films in Review*, March/April 1995

Thomson, David, *A Biographical Dictionary of Film*, Andre Deutsch, London, 1995

– – – 'The Alien Quartet', *Bloomsbury Movie Guide*, no. 4, Bloomsbury, London, 1998

Walker, Mark (ed.), *Gramophone Film Music Good CD Guide*, Gramophone Publications Limited, Harrow, Middlesex, 1998

Wright, Adrian, *Arnold Schwarzenegger: A Life on Film*, Robert Hale, London, 1994

cinematic terms

auteur the notion that a film's director can be considered as its author. By studying a director's output, particular themes and styles can be seen to run through most, if not all, of their films

B-movie a motion picture film made to be shown as a comparison to a main feature. B-movies were made on low budgets, usually with lesser-known stars, and often with formulaic plots

dailies or rushes the first positive prints, usually synchronised with sound, 'rushed' back from the laboratory and viewed in a raw unedited form. This film is used primarily for checking all facets of shooting

diegesis the narrative world created by the film. Everything that exists in the film's world is part of the diegesis; anything represented as coming from a source outside of this world, such as credits and music that the characters cannot hear, is non-diegetic

establishing shot often the opening shot of a sequence, which establishes location but can also establish mood or give the viewer information concerning the time and general situation. Establishing shots generally are long shots or extreme long shots

exploitation film a low budget film that exploits a subject for commercial advantage by pandering to the curiosity of the audience. The term often describes especially violent and crudely sexual films

film noir a term used to describe a particular kind of film made by the Hollywood studios during the late 1940s and early 1950s. The world of film noir is often a dark, brutal and violent urban world of crime and corruption. The style of such films emphasises bleak settings, heavy shadows and sharp contrasts of light and dark

flashback a shot, scene or sequence that takes place at some other time, most often the past, outside of the present time established in the film. The Terminator employs the use of what Cameron terms future flashbacks, as the time travelling Reese has a different sense of time having come from the future to the present – 1984 Los Angeles

mise-en-scène literally, in the picture; how all of the elements within the frame interact in order to create meaning

pan shot a shot in which the camera moves horizontally around a fixed axis to survey an area

parallel action action taking place at two or more locations at the same time or occurring at different times, and shown alternately on the screen with the camera parallel cutting from one location to the other

shot a series of images produced by continuous filming from a single camera. This is the basic building block of film

tracking shot any shot in which the camera is moved to follow the movement of a subject

credits

production companies

Cinema 84

A Greenberg Brothers Partnership
A Pacific Western Production
A Euro Film Funding Ltd. Feature
An Orion Pictures Release

director

James Cameron

executive producers

John Daly, Derek Gibson

producer

Gale Anne Hurd

screenplay

James Cameron,
Gale Anne Hurd

director of photography

Adam Greenberg

editor

Mark Goldblatt

art director

George Costello

music

Brad Fiedel

special visual effects photographer

John Huneck

special visual effects

Fantasy II Film Effects (production
supervisor Leslie Huntley)

additional dialogue

William Wisher Jnr

colour process

CFI; Prints by DeLuxe

rear screen projectionist

Gerald McClain

opticals

Ray Mercer and Company, (effects)
Image 3, Laurel Klick, Phil Huff,
(consultant) Mark Sawicki

matte artist

Ken Marschall

graphic animation effects

Ernest D. Farino

special effects supervisor

Gene Warren Jnr

pyrotechnics and fire effects

Joseph Viskocil

costume design

Hilary Wright, (supervisor)
Deborah Everton

credits

title design
Ernest D. Farino

cast

Terminator –
Arnold Schwarzenegger

Kyle Reese – Michael Biehn

Sarah Connor – Linda Hamilton

Traxler – Paul Winfield

Vukovich – Lance Henriksen

Matt – Rick Rossovich

Ginger – Bess Motta

Silberman – Earl Boen

Pawn shop clerk – Dick Miller

Punk leader – Bill Paxton

Punks – Brad Rearden,
Brian Thompson

Other titles in the series

Other titles available in the York Film Notes series:

Title	ISBN
8½ (Otto e mezzo)	0582 40488 6
A bout de souffle	0582 43182 4
Apocalypse Now	0582 43183 2
Battleship Potemkin	0582 40490 8
Blade Runner	0582 43198 0
Casablanca	0582 43200 6
Chinatown	0582 43199 9
Citizen Kane	0582 40493 2
Das Cabinet des Dr Caligari	0582 40494 0
Double Indemnity	0582 43196 4
Dracula	0582 43197 2
Easy Rider	0582 43195 6
Fargo	0582 43193 X
Fear Eats the Soul	0582 48224 3
La Haine	0582 43194 8
Lawrence of Arabia	0582 43192 1
Psycho	0582 43191 3
Pulp Fiction	0582 40510 7
Romeo and Juliet	0582 43189 1
Some Like It Hot	0582 40503 3
Stagecoach	0582 43187 5
Taxi Driver	0582 40506 8
The Full Monty	0582 43181 6
The Godfather	0582 43188 3
The Piano	0582 43190 5
The Searchers	0582 40510 6
The Third Man	0582 40511 4
Thelma and Louise	0582 43184 0
Unforgiven	0582 43185 9

Also from York Notes

Also available in the **York Notes** range:

York Notes

The ultimate literature guides for GCSE students (or equivalent levels)

York Notes Advanced

Literature guides for A-level and undergraduate students (or equivalent levels)

York Personal Tutors

Personal tutoring on essential GCSE English and Maths topics

Available from good bookshops.

For full details, please visit our website at www.longman-yorknotes.com

notes

notes

notes

notes